ACKNOWLEDGMENTS

Thank you to Craig and Emilie Wierda and Rod and Libby VanSolkema from Ancient Paths for making the trips to Israel possible and to Elisa Moed from Travelujah for arranging so many transformative meetings. Emilie Wierda, Dan Zimmerman, David Nekrutman from the Isaiah Projects, Gordon Middleton from Patrick Henry College, and the Summit Ministries publishing team made this a much better book through their excellent feedback. Matthew Faraci and Chris McIntire from Gideon 300 have helped spread the word far beyond anything I could have imagined. This book would never have happened without the love, bravery, and support of the incomparable Stephanie Myers.

The viewpoints expressed in this book are the result of personal study, interviews, conversations, and prayer. They should not be construed as constituting an official position of Summit Ministries or its board.

SHOULD CHRISTIANS SUPPORT ISRAEL?

Seeking a Biblical Worldview in an Impossible Situation

Jeff Myers, Ph.D.

Published by Summit Ministries
PO Box 207
Manitou Springs, CO 80829

ISBN 978-1-957406-41-1
Printed in the United States of America

summit.org/israel

Summit Ministries exists to equip the rising generation to understand and live out their Christian convictions in today's culture. We help young Christians—and those who work with young Christians—engage today's tough issues such as abortion, transgenderism, relativism, competing worldviews, critical theory, justice, and other cultural ideas influencing the next generation.

Support Summit's mission by donating or requesting more books to help share truth with the rising generation. Scan the QR code to get started.

TABLE OF CONTENTS

PART I

WHY YOU SHOULD **CARE** ABOUT ISRAEL

CHAPTER I

The Gates of Gaza

1150 BCE, Day Unknown
Midnight

Samson rose from the bed of the Gazan prostitute who had entertained him the night before. He needed to leave *now* before the Gazans sprang their trap. In a fury, Samson ripped out the city's gates and gateposts, hoisted them on his shoulders, and carried them to a hill overlooking Hebron—thirty-six miles away (Judges 16).

Hebron is the final resting place of Judaism's founder, Abraham. It was settled by Caleb, who earned his place in the land by defeating the vaunted giants, whose presence terrified the Israelites into forfeiting the territory God had promised (Judges 14). By carrying the heavy gates of Gaza to Hebron, Samson symbolically stripped away the defenses of

Israel's tormentors, delivering his enemies to the bosom of Abraham. It was a grunting and violent act of prophecy, a superhuman feat in which a degenerate patriarch symbolically offered up his enemies at the grave of a redeemed patriarch, the one whose willingness to sacrifice his own son foreshadowed the coming Messiah. A hundred years later, Samson's prophecy came true when a shepherd boy named David defeated the giant Goliath, leading to a rout of the Philistine army of Gaza.

April 29, 1956
Sunrise

Roi Rotberg was on patrol. At sunrise, the twenty-one-year-old from Tel Aviv rode on horseback, guarding the fields surrounding the Nahal Oz kibbutz. Roi was an idealist. He desired peace with the Palestinians and with mankind. The kibbutz's communal mission filled him with hope.

Off in the distance, Roi saw some Arabs illegally picking produce from the kibbutz's fields. He rode over to shoo them away. It was a trap. Infiltrators from Gaza shot and killed Roi, then horribly mutilated his corpse.

"But beyond the furrow that marks the border, lies a surging sea of hatred and vengeance, yearning for the day that the tranquility blunts our alertness" –Moshe Dayan

The following day, the tiny community of Nahal Oz gathered to mourn Roi's death. Moshe Dayan, the Israeli Defense Force's chief of staff, offered a short speech—just 238 words long. It quickly became Israel's version of Abraham Lincoln's *Gettysburg Address*.

Dayan's words, like Lincoln's, were prophetic: "But beyond the furrow that marks the border, lies a surging sea of hatred and vengeance, yearning for the day that the tranquility blunts our alertness, for the day that we heed the ambassadors of conspiring hypocrisy, who call for us to lay down our arms."

And with a reference to Samson, Dayan concluded, "Roi—the light in his heart blinded his eyes and he saw not the flash of the blade. The longing for peace deafened his ears and he heard not the sound of the coiled murderers. The gates of Gaza were too heavy for his shoulders, and they crushed him."[1]

October 7, 2023
Sunrise

Hamas terrorists broke through the gates dividing Israel from Gaza. Swarming into Nahal Oz and other unsuspecting Israeli communities, they chopped off their victims' breasts, genitals, arms, and feet and shot, burned, tortured, raped, and beheaded them.[2] Israelis fought for their very lives; but by the end of the day, an unfathomable twelve hundred of them had been slaughtered.

Hamas had rehearsed their military campaign for two years.[3] Its terrorists attacked with bestial ferocity, fueled by a highly addictive amphetamine called Captagon.[4] [5] But drugs alone don't explain this brutality. These terrorists had been raised to hate Jews, to learn how to kill them, and to relish the day they might be unleashed to bring about a bloody reckoning. They learned this in schools sponsored by the United Nations and funded by international donors, including the United States. For three decades, Hamas indoctrinated Gazans with the promise of deliverance but instead brutishly tightened their bonds. It had only one aim: annihilate Israel.

> For three decades Hamas indoctrinated Gazans with the promise of deliverance but instead brutishly tightened their bonds. It had only one aim: annihilate Israel.

On October 7, 2023, scores of Jews were killed, as well as seventeen Arabs, including a nine-months-pregnant Bedouin woman wearing a hijab. Thirty-three US citizens were also killed. The terrorists took nearly 250 hostages of twenty nationalities and five different religions. Among them were several elderly people and a small baby. Hamas imprisoned its captives in a network of tunnels built to facilitate military action and store weapons. Some of the hostages were released. Others were killed. As of this writing, ninety-nine of the remaining hostages are thought to still be alive.

I have seen the evidence of the massacre. I've spent time listening to the firsthand testimonies of those who were there. The Hamas terrorists themselves documented the attack in real time with gun-mounted cameras and through social media posts. They wanted the world to know. They wanted everyone—Jews especially—to live eternally with the knowledge that Hamas would never relent in its demented aims.

Amnesty International's Secretary General Agnès Callamard, who accuses Israel of war crimes on the daily, admitted that Hamas's butchery displayed a "chilling disregard for human life."[6] Disregard? No. For Hamas, the butchery was intentional. Hamas is not a group of street thugs. It is a highly disciplined and hierarchically organized army. Its slaughter was a carefully planned tactic, serving the strategic aim of turning the world against Israel. So far, it has worked.

> The October 7 attack was about everything, everywhere—a pitched battle between worldviews involving issues of God, justice, force... and the nature of truth itself.

When we're in conflict, what it's about is never what it's about. The October 7 attack was not, as Hamas's narrative frames it, an act of self-defense in the name of resistance. It was not, as Hamas's Western apologists would have us believe, an unfortunate overreach in a cross-border skirmish. It is about everything, everywhere—a pitched battle between worldviews involving issues of God, justice, force, genocide, oppression, corruption, religion, and the nature of truth itself. This is not just geopolitical. It is theopolitical.

The Theopolitical Struggle over Israel's Legitimacy

Geopolitics is about territory. Theopolitics is about ideology. The word "theopolitical" doesn't even appear in my dictionary. It should. A geopolitical struggle can be solved by slightly redrawing borders and offering financial stipends to ease the indignity of compromise. Theopolitical struggles, on the other hand, are not so easily solved. They are both spiritual and material. Vastly divergent views of God and society are at play. Territorial concessions alone cannot solve an ideological conflict.

Ideology is the study of ideas. We live in a world of ideas—bad ones as well as good ones. Bad ideas spread like viruses. They flood our minds and hearts, causing us to question God, truth, and even reality itself. Bad ideas are the deadliest things on earth.

Exhibit A in the war of ideas is the Second World War. In Germany, it was Nazism; in Italy, fascism; in Japan, imperialism. Millions died in battle, but noncombatants suffered the most—tens of millions of civilians shot, gassed, bombed, or killed by war-related starvation and disease. With the rise of communist governments in Russia and China, the suffering multiplied beyond any human ability to comprehend. Possibly 150 million people died at the hands of their communist over-lords, more than all the people victimized by all wars up to that point in human history.[7] The communists' theopolitical aim of killing God and ruling humanity led them to rule as gods and kill humanity.

Hamas's tactics draw from the same playbook. Its ends are served by any means. Mere death does not satisfy its blood lust. Hamas is an ecstatically revivalist cult that seeks to purify itself by defiling those it opposes. It desecrates victims not only to defeat them but also to deplete their lives of meaning. In halting English, one Israeli Defense Force (IDF) soldier perfectly encapsulated Hamas's aims: "They didn't just want to kill us. They wanted to un-holy us."[8]

Hamas is not satisfied with immolating Jews. It wants to incite the whole world against them. Even as it unleashed terror on unsuspecting Israeli communities, its public relations arm unleashed mind viruses to sear the consciences of seemingly intelligent, caring people the world over. To a shocking degree, Hamas succeeded, especially with Gen Z. A majority of young adults seamlessly transitioned from concern for the Palestinian's plight to an open embrace of Hamas's plainly stated genocidal aims. Ugly antisemitism was served up as justice, wanton vengeance as self-defense. The earth's moral poles, already unstable, shifted in a day. What ideology was behind this?

> Bad ideas spread like viruses. They flood our minds and hearts, causing us to question God, truth, and even reality itself. Bad ideas are the deadliest things on earth.

Jew Hatred Exposed

While most Americans have consistently expressed support for Israel, polls reveal a society-wide rift, not between political parties or religions but between generations. An April 2024 Summit Ministries/RMG Research poll revealed that young adults eighteen to twenty-four are more than three times as likely as the general population to deny that Israel even has a right to exist.[9]

A Harvard/CAPS poll two weeks after October 7 revealed that 51 percent of Gen Z agreed that "the killing of 1200 Israeli civilians and the kidnapping of another 250 civilians can be justified by the grievances of Palestinians."[10] By December, that figure had risen to 60 percent.[11]

> Gen Z readily admitted that Hamas is a murderous terrorist group yet also agreed that the brutal killing of innocent Israelis was justified because of Palestinian grievances.

Even before October 7, there were disturbing signs that anti-Jewish and anti-Israel sentiment are more popular among Gen Z than any other beliefs, with the possible exceptions of unrestricted abortion and socialism. The Anti-Defamation League (ADL) says that reports of antisemitic behavior are at the highest number since ADL began charting such incidents in 1979.[12] In recent days, Jewish students have reported enduring antisemitic slurs in class, being expelled from campus clubs, and having swastikas carved into the walls of their rooms.[13] According to *USA Today*, at the Ivy League Cornell University, posts to the university's Greekrank forum threatened to "rape female Jewish students and behead Jewish babies in front of their parents," and another called for students to follow Jewish students home from campus and slit their throats."[14]

Many Americans suspect that universities are becoming toxic waste dumps of spent ideas. But terrorist sympathizing? Isn't that overly dramatic? Not according to the journalist Khaled Abu Toameh. Toameh is an Arab Muslim and highly respected correspondent on Palestinian affairs. He told a group of leaders, of which I was a part, that he has felt safer interviewing the PLO and Hamas leadership than he does giving lectures at US colleges. "There is more support for Hamas on US campuses than among Arabs in Israel," Toameh said. "Not even the Palestinian territory of the West Bank hosts parades like those seen on US campuses."[15]

> There is more support for Hamas on US campuses than among Arabs in Israel."
> –Khaled Abu Toameh

After the October 7 attack, things went so far that TikTok videos that venerated 9/11 mastermind Osama bin Laden began multiplying. Young adults from all walks of life expressed their admiration for bin Laden's "Letter to America" and testified of their newfound appreciation for terrorism as a justified tool of resistance against Western power.

Hamas is counting on the support of the rising generation of Americans. They are getting it. Within days of the October 7 attack, Hamas was hosting rallies on American campuses. These soon spilled out onto the streets, where marchers chanted, "From the river to the sea, Palestine will be free." It is a clever rhyme curated for an English-speaking audience.

Why do tens of thousands of people, most of whom have no idea of what river and sea they're chanting about, join in these protests? Young Americans instinctively sympathize with the underdog. This sympathy is easily manipulated. The names of the river and the sea don't matter to them. They just see a marginalized group in want of support and never consider the ideological corral into which they are being herded.

Hamas's endgame is not a secret. At a rally in Dearborn, Michigan, headlined by the city's mayor, a former congressional aid called President Biden a "cancer" for supporting Israel and led the crowd in chanting "Genocide Joe." The publisher of an Arab newspaper announced to the zealous crowd, "We are on the road to a great victory here in D.C. and there in Palestine."[16] The co-master of ceremonies, Lexis Zeidan, said to the crowd, "Remember it doesn't end at a ceasefire. A ceasefire is the bare minimum. It ends when we see the dismantling of the terrorist racist state of Israel, and a free, free Palestine."[17]

> Americans instinctively sympathize with the underdog. This sympathy is easily manipulated.

What constitutes victory to Hamas and its supporters? The annihilation of the Jewish state of Israel. In pursuit of this aim, Hamas leaders take great aid and comfort from their American support. Khaled Mashaal, a Hamas leader who has become a billionaire by skimming off international aid coming into Gaza, gloated that student rallies have "revived that dream" among Hamas leaders.[18]

Gen Z isn't as much pro-Palestinian as it is anti-Israel. A *New York Times* poll in December showed that Gen Z consistently sees Israel as unserious about peace and an intentional killer of civilians, an evil power unworthy of US support.[19]

What Is a Biblical Worldview in an Impossible Situation?

My concern over Hamas's indoctrination of American young adults inspired an opinion-editorial piece for *The Daily Wire* just before Thanksgiving 2023. My guess was that a potent virus of postmodernism, anti-Americanism, and moral relativism had infected young adults. I titled the op-ed, "Congratulations, America: You've Raised a Generation of Terrorist Sympathizers," and wrote, "Is anyone surprised that a generation this untethered from reality might cheer for a terrorist group such as Hamas?" I quoted Voltaire: "Surely whoever can get them to believe absurdities can get them to commit atrocities."

> This book is not about dismissing the plight of the Palestinians. It is not about endorsing Israel's every action. It is about seeking a biblical worldview in an impossible situation.

This book is an expansion of that op-ed. It is not about dismissing the plight of the Palestinians. It is not about endorsing Israel's every action. It is about seeking a biblical worldview in an impossible situation.

My conviction is that a biblical worldview—as a workable account of reality itself—has the power not only to explain reality but also to promote blessing and flourishing. To demonstrate how this applies to the Israel/Palestine conflict, we will explore the following:

- the indoctrination that is taking place,
- the war between competing worldviews,
- the history of Israel and Palestine and the worldviews behind them,
- the tactics of the apocalyptic rape-and-death cult called Hamas,
- the nature of just war and genocide,
- how the world might move forward based on a biblical worldview, and
- lessons in resilience and hope for our time.

Coming to a knowledge of the truth and taking appropriate action is what this book is about.

My search for the truth about Israel led me to join a small group of leaders on a wartime visit to Israel. It was just 103 days after October 7. There, we met with journalists, educators, military officials, an intelligence officer, survivors, and hostage families. We met with Jews and Arabs, with people on the left and on the right, and with peace activists and soldiers. What we learned is not at all what I expected.

CHAPTER 2

Israel in **Wartime**—A Firsthand Account

An Israeli security agent at JFK disabused me of the notion that getting into Israel during a time of war wouldn't be that different than my previous trips. She sifted through every item in my suitcase and backpack, asking probing questions. "Why are you going to Israel now? Don't you know we are at war?"

Arriving at Tel Aviv's nearly empty Ben Gurion Airport, I was once again questioned. This time, I was ready.

"I'm on a solidarity mission," I said.

The passport agent fired back, "Solidarity with *whom*?" and shoved the stamped passport back across the counter without waiting for an answer.

The tension expressed by that passport agent was evident everywhere, even in the oddly quiet streets of Jerusalem, where the flow of pilgrims (usually two million a year) had slowed to a trickle.

In Jerusalem, the members of our group came together in a hotel conference room to learn about the state of the war from an intelligence officer named Itamar Ben David. He surprised us by asking if he could open the meeting with a prayer of blessing from the book of Numbers:

> Y'varekh'khah Adonai V'yishm'rekha.
> Ya'eir Adonai panav eilekha vihuneka.
> Yisa Adonai panav eilekha v'yaseim l'kha shalom.

In English, it says:

> May God bless you and keep you.
> May God cause God's spirit to shine upon you and be
>   gracious unto you.
> May God turn God's spirit unto you and grant you peace.[20]

Itamar's lips quivered as he led us into this holy moment. I recalled a Shabbat dinner with a Jewish friend in which I placed my hands on the heads of my two sons and recited this blessing over them.

The discussion was lively—polite but pointed questions, equally straightforward responses. In fact, all our meetings were this way. To a person, those we met shared their thoughts and feelings without compunction. Many offered blunt assessments of the current military and political situation. All expressed gratitude that people from the US would come to personally hear them out.

Early the next morning, we hopped on a bus with our security guard and rode to the southern part of the country. Within an hour and a half from Jerusalem, we neared the Gaza border. Artillery shells flew overhead. Across farm fields, we could see clouds of smoke arising from Gaza as the IDF targeted terrorist hideouts. The road suddenly became rough, chewed up by tank treads.

This rural and agricultural part of Israel reminded me of Missouri or Oklahoma or, perhaps, California's Central valley, except for the bomb shelters dotting the highways like bus stops. Many of these were colorfully painted, as if to smile them up a bit and disguise their purpose of sheltering travelers from Hamas's death-dealing rocket attacks. We were so close to the border that if Hamas did fire a rocket at us, we were told we would have seven seconds to take shelter. Residents there have built safe rooms designed to withstand rocket and mortar fire. For many families, these safe rooms become children's bedrooms; so the kids don't have to figure out what to do in a terrifying situation. Most of the safe rooms did not have locks. Why would they? Rockets don't attack through doors.

Soon, we arrived at Kfar Aza, a tiny agrarian community called a kibbutz. Surrounded by a razor wire-topped fence, Kfar Aza was once a bustling neighborhood consisting of a plastics business, a school, a clinic, a community center, and modest homes. It was empty, except for our group of civilians and squads of soldiers touring the devastation. We donned body armor and Kevlar helmets, a weighty reminder that we were in an active war zone.

Our guide, Chen Kotler, a local resident, shared her heartbreaking experience from October 7. Early in the morning, seventy Hamas terrorists had penetrated the compound from four directions and from paragliders. They stormed through the streets, shooting and killing anyone they encountered, launching rocket-propelled grenades into homes and burning alive those barricaded in their safe rooms. Sixty-five people perished.

The homes were riddled with bullet holes. Many showed evidence of explosions and fires. Each home featured spray-painted markings listing the date the building had been cleared. A red circle with a dot in the middle denoted whether a body had been found inside. Nearly every home had a red circle. One of them had been home to the community's doctor, his wife, and twin ten-month-old children. Both the doctor and his wife were shot and killed by the terrorists. For fourteen hours, the babies cried for their parents. Anyone who tried to come to their rescue was gunned down.

The redness of the spray-painted markings called to mind the Passover in Egypt, when the blood-marked doorposts saved the Israelites from death. There was no passing over here. Death had visited nearly every home. Our group reverently walked the streets, trying to get our minds around the slaughter that had taken place here just weeks before. Why had this happened? Were these attackers animals? How could they have so viciously attacked this peaceful community? How could the residents have been so caught off guard, knowing all they knew about Hamas's stated intention of killing as many Jews as possible?

Back on the bus, our normally verbal group rode in silence. Soon we arrived at the city of Sderot, where forty people had been murdered, including a group of senior citizens on a minibus. Terrorists there had specifically targeted the police station, killing twenty officers. We gathered in the temporary police headquarters and watched sickening video footage of the attack from the city's CCTV cameras.

Of all the videos and photos I've seen of bodies, blood, and burned vehicles, nothing affected me as much as the CCTV footage of terrorists shooting the vehicle of a fleeing family. Our group watched in horror as a father flung open the door of the car, grabbed a child, and fled down the street in an awkward shuffle, body bent as a shield. Suddenly, gunfire felled him. The child jumped up and ran back down the street, her tiny hands covering her ears as she desperately searched for her mother.

As we watched clips of the attack, I studied the impassive faces of the police station employees. I didn't blame them for being shut down emotionally. How much devastation and bloodshed can one person take? What was it like to be charged with people's safety and find yourself completely helpless to save them? With Gaza just a three-minute drive away, when would the next attack come? In an hour? A day? A year? Would this go on forever?

A short drive later, we arrived at the gate of a military installation called Re'im. An IDF major boarded the bus to give us a briefing. "We are pushing Hamas back and don't expect an attack; but if one comes, drop down wherever you are, lay flat, and put your hands over the back of your neck. You'll have less than ten seconds."

The major, we soon learned, was a reservist named Nir Boms. He casually mentioned that in civilian life, he served as a professor at Tel Aviv University. I looked him up later—*Doctor* Nir Boms, a famous professor who spoke around the world and wrote scholarly articles in English, Hebrew, and Arabic.

Wow, I thought. *Everyone here steps up; one must be a person of action as well as a person of thought.*

Re'im was a mess. On October 7, forty terrorists overwhelmed the gates and slaughtered everyone they could find. I have never seen so many bullet holes—hundreds. As the terrorists attacked Re'im, a small handful of soldiers had bravely confronted them. These soldiers, I later discovered, were Bedouin Muslims. One group of Muslims fought to preserve Israel; one group of Muslims fought to destroy it.

Later, under Major Bom's guidance, our group visited the site of the Nova Music Festival, where terrorists murdered hundreds more Israelis, systematically gang-raping, shooting, mutilating, and burning alive their victims. Our civilian and military guides struggled to communicate what they had witnessed. Their descriptions seemed robotic at times.

I wondered, *How many times had they had to relive the nightmare for visiting dignitaries?*

We ended the evening at a kibbutz called Mefalsim, a staging area for an elite IDF reserve force assembled just the week before to ensure the safety of returning citizens. There, we helped serve at a barbecue for reservists. At dinner, I sat next to a soldier named Alex. His rifle barrel pointed upward and occasionally wavered in my direction, which made me nervous. Hadn't he taken a safe hunter course and learned about muzzle control? It was hard to remember that just a week before, he had been a civilian, like me.

"What do you do in your civilian life, Alex?"

"I am—how do you say it?—a train driver."

"Engineer. That's what we call it in the US," I said.

He laughed. "I am not an engineer. I just drive."

Alex and I talked about his experience in the war. He struck me as completely open, willing to answer all my questions. When he didn't know the answer, he called for help from the other soldiers seated around. We talked about faith, and Alex showed me a small icon he carried in his pocket—a gift from his father, who was a Christian.

Our conversation was interrupted when two reservists with a keyboard and a saxophone struck up a lively tune. Within seconds, everyone was clapping and singing along, especially when they got to the chorus, which in English is:

This is my home; this is my heart.
And I will not leave you,
Our ancestors, our roots.
We are the flowers, the melodies,
Sitting as brothers and sisters.

Out of the corner of my eye, I saw Dr. Nir Bom, the reserve major, dancing along with a silly shuffle.

Suddenly, a reservist with gray hair strode up to the keyboardist for a loud exchange. The music stopped. The soldiers fell into an embarrassed silence.

Before storming out of the tent, the man shouted something in Hebrew. I asked a Hebrew-speaking friend to translate. "He says, 'It is not a time for joy with 136 of our community not here. Keep the noise down.'"

Immediately, the musicians switched to a somber tune—a prayer, really—one that is recited in unison at the synagogue every Monday and Thursday. In English, it says:

As for our brothers,
The whole house of Israel
Who are given over to trouble or captivity,
Whether they abide on the sea or the dry land:
May the All-present have mercy upon them,
And bring them forth from trouble to enlargement,
From darkness to light,
And from subjection to redemption,
Now speedily and at a near time.

After a bit, I wandered back outside and came across an IDF soldier I had connected with earlier in the day.

"Do you want an espresso?" he asked.

"No, I think I'll have a hard enough time getting to sleep tonight. But I'll go with you."

He opened the back of his van and fired up a small Nespresso machine just like the one I have at home. While I waited for him to finish, I helped my friend David Nekrutman stow two large boxes of socks in the van. David and his wife, Kalanit, have worked tirelessly to meet the needs of the reservists and other Israelis affected by the war. The soldiers were thrilled with the socks. It's amazing what counts as a thoughtful gift when you've suddenly left home and found yourself away for three months.

The soldier climbed down out of his van, espresso in hand. I shivered in the cold and sort of wished I had taken him up on his offer. We talked about his experience in the war. Some of what he shared I am not going to tell you

> "People say the terrorists who did this weren't human, that they were beasts. It isn't true. They were humans just like us. But they believed a lie and went to a dark place." –IDF soldier

because it was disturbing beyond what I feel capable of describing in this book. But one statement I will remember forever.

"People say the terrorists who did this weren't human, that they were beasts." The soldier paused to take a sip of coffee. "It isn't true. They were humans just like us. But they believed a lie and went to a dark place."

All we like sheep have gone astray, I recalled from Isaiah.[21] Certainly, there are levels of evil. But there is no one who is innocent, no, not one. *Lord, have mercy.* It reminded me of Alexandr Solzhenitsyn's lament in *Gulag Archipelago,* a voluminous account of evil in the Soviet system: "the line dividing good and evil cuts through the heart of every human being."[22]

It was late, and we ran out of words. Shaking hands, I offered a quick blessing I hoped would encourage him and wandered back to the meal tent. Dinner was over, and the music had stopped; but many reservists remained behind to chat with our group.

One of the soldiers—a computer scientist working for a prestigious company in civilian life—took me aside. He pulled out his phone, showing me a picture of a beautiful young woman.

"Her name is Shani Louk," he said. "I work with her mother. Shani was at the festival. After Hamas attacked, her mother begged me to find her daughter." He paused, looking me in the eyes. "I did not find her. But I found part of her skull. No one can live when they lose that part of their skull. I had to tell her mother that Shani is no longer with us."

The soldier put his phone back in his pocket. We stood quietly for a moment. What could I say? Anger flashed briefly in his eyes, settling into a deep sadness.

Finally, he said, "This is why we do what we do."

I didn't talk to anyone on the bus ride back to our hotel. That's not like me. But what more was there to talk about? What we had seen, we couldn't unsee. What we had heard, we couldn't unhear.

I pulled out my journal and tapped on the overhead light. I had a responsibility—a duty—to process, to pray, and to tell the truth. Over the next few weeks, that search led me to explore the birth of the nation that is at the heart of the conflict we now face.

CHAPTER 3

The Israel You Haven't **Heard** About

The modern nation of Israel is tiny, with a land size just over 1 percent of that of its archenemy, Iran. Half of Israel's territory is barren desert, sparsely populated by Bedouin tribes and farmers. Nine million citizens live in the remaining areas. About two million of them are Arabs. A small percentage is Christian. The rest, about seven million, are Jews. About half of Israel's Jews are secular.

Given that so many of Israel's Jews are not religious, we must ask: What is a Jew? Is Judaism a religion? An ethnic identity? A set of cultural practices? Let's take a moment for a thumbnail history before we go on.

In Scripture, Judah (Yehuda in Hebrew) was the oldest son of Jacob, whom God had renamed Israel. After their return from exile in Babylon, those who made up the people group known as Israel were called Jews, in deference to the nation's dominant tribe, Judah. Judaism is the creed of these people. It is based on the Hebrew Bible (the Tanakh) and subsequent revered writings and interpretations.

Judaism is both a set of beliefs and practices, as well as a cultural identity that was once ethnically singular but has become ethnically diverse. In Israel, there are migrants from 103 countries, speaking eighty-two different languages. This defies the "white settler colonialist" label with which Israel's citizens—and Jews everywhere—are smeared.

The Jews are the only people group to have ever established a nation state in the now disputed land, and they did so more than three thousand years ago. Since the overthrow of Jerusalem by Rome in AD 70, though, the land has been ruled by foreign capitals as an administrative district. This was true until the 1940s when Israel and its surrounding nations came into existence in their present form.

Israel is bordered on all sides by Muslim nations: Lebanon, Syria, Jordan, and Egypt. Lebanon and Syria are openly hostile to Israel. Lebanon is the home of the terrorist group Hezbollah—fully funded by Iran—which boasts perhaps a hundred thousand fighters and a hundred thousand missiles aimed at Israel. To the south and east of Israel are Jordan and Egypt. Both have been hostile in the past. At the present time, their relations are tense yet stable. Two Palestinian territories also border Israel—Gaza, and the West Bank. Both are ruled by groups that openly deny Israel's right to exist.

> The Jews are the only people group to have ever established a nation state in the land, and they did so more than three thousand years ago.

Some people will say, "Well, the modern state of Israel wasn't formed until 1948! It's not legitimate!" Irrelevant. None of the modern states in the region existed in their present form until well after the breakup of the Ottoman Empire in the early 1900s. Lebanon, Israel's neighbor to the north, was formed in 1943. Syria, Israel's neighbor to the northeast, was formed in 1944. Jordan, Israel's neighbor to the east, was formed in 1946. Egypt, Israel's neighbor to the south, became an independent nation in 1947. Why wasn't a Palestinian state formed at that same time? The Palestinian Arabs involved in the negotiations refused to form one—then or ever since.

Of these newly created states, only Israel has a claim to the land extending back to antiquity. Jews trace their history back to passages such as Genesis 18, when the Lord visited Abraham and promised his offspring would be a great nation. Four hundred thirty years transpired between that promise and the Exodus from Egypt. From the time of the Exodus—possibly around 1300 BCE—Jews have lived in the land, even though the modern state of Israel was not officially recognized by the United Nations until 1948.

> Why wasn't a Palestinian state formed in 1948? Because the Palestinian Arabs involved in the negotiations refused to form one—then or ever since.

Israel is the world's only Jewish state. By comparison, there are fifty-seven member states of the Organization of the Islamic Conference. About 1.8 billion people in the world are Muslim. The total number of Jews in the world is just over fifteen million. For every Jew in the world, there are 120 Muslims. Most Muslims today have an unfavorable view of Jews. In Lebanon, for example, 99 percent of the population views Jews unfavorably.[23] This puts Israel in a nearly impossible situation. It is surrounded by hostile forces adhering to a worldview that has, over the centuries, become hostile to Judaism itself. Even in the "less hostile" neighboring countries, Jordan and Egypt, 95 percent of the population view Jews unfavorably.

It isn't only the surrounding nations that isolate Israel. On my recent fact-finding mission, Rabbi Doron Perez told our group in frustration, "Israel is the only one of the 193 member nations of the United Nations whose right to exist is regularly challenged."

He's correct. In 2023, the United Nations General Assembly adopted twenty-one condemnations. Two were against Russia. The United States, North Korea, Iran, Syria, and Myanmar each received one. The other fourteen were all condemnations of Israel, for everything from Israel's occupation of the Golan Heights as a buffer against Syrian military action to a war-related oil spill eighteen years ago.[24]

Since 2015, the UN has passed 140 resolutions against Israel and only sixty-eight against all other countries combined.[25] A hundred sixty or more of the world's nations regularly join in these resolutions. To be sure, Israel's actions are viewed by the world with a special kind of negativity. For example, neighboring Syria killed 1.2 million people between

2021 and 2023. This is twenty-four times as many Palestinians as have died in wars with Israel in its entire seventy-five-year history. Yet when I googled "Israeli atrocities," there were four times as many results as when I googled "Syrian atrocities." It leaves the impression that no matter what Israel does, it will be covered four times as negatively.

Given the constant hostility Israel faces, the world's tiny population of Jews, and the Holocaust, which killed more than half of Europe's Jews in the 1930s and 1940s, you can imagine why Jews see a homeland as vital to their very existence and why they so strongly assert Israel's right to exist. Broadly speaking, "Zionism" is the term that both Jews and non-Jews use to refer to this right.

Israel is unique among nations. Itamar Ben David, the Israeli intelligence officer I mentioned earlier, described Israel to our group as not as much a religious nation as a nation with a Divine constitution. The constitutional republic framework given by God to Moses has become the basis of constitutional governments around the world. Harvard University professor Eric Nelson says that the American Constitution was specifically designed to incorporate elements of the Hebrew republic. If the Hebrews, under the leadership of Moses, had established a different kind of government, we might very well not have anything resembling the freedoms we enjoy today in America.[26]

"Israel is the only one of the 193 member nations of the United Nations whose right to exist is regularly challenged." –Rabbi Doron Perez

According to Ben David, the aspiration of this ancient Divine constitution can be summarized in two words: *tzedaqah*, a state of society in which justice reigns, and *mishpat*, what is needed to restore justice from injustice.[27] The Old Testament chronicles a great deal of injustice, both on the part of Israel and its enemies, and efforts to restore justice through military conquest, political development, and religious revival.

Because of its unique place in history and its unique relationship with God, Judaism is a lightning rod among the nations. Some people love the Jews. Many, many more hate them and everything they stand for. Hardly anyone is neutral. In his history of the Jews, Paul Johnson says that Jews are "exemplars and epitomizers of the human condition. They seemed to present all the inescapable dilemmas of man in a heightened and clarified form."[28]

The tensions of humanity are present inside the state of Israel as much as outside. Inside the nation, there are four "tribes": ultra-Orthodox Jews, religious Jews, secular Jews, and Arabs. Each of these maintains distinct lifestyles, neighborhoods, and, for the most part, schools. The American ideal of a "melting pot" is nowhere visible in Israel. Tension between the four groups is managed, not resolved.

> "Jews are fiercely individualistic. At times this makes them unconquerable. It also makes them almost ungovernable, almost impossible to lead."
> –Rabbi Jonathan Sacks

The late Jonathan Sacks, a widely admired rabbi, admitted, "Jews are fiercely individualistic. At times this makes them unconquerable. It also makes them almost ungovernable, almost impossible to lead."[29] It has been this way for millennia. When Moses tried to intervene in a fight between two Hebrew slaves, one of them confronted him by asking, "Who made you ruler and judge over us?" (Exodus 2:14).

The political situation in Israel exemplifies this individualistic attitude. Whereas there are fewer than a dozen political parties in the United States, with only the Democratic and Republican parties having significant membership, there are fifty-five political parties in Israel. Fifteen of these hold seats in Israel's governing body, the Knesset. As of this writing, the largest of these parties, Likud, only holds thirty-two seats out of the 120 available and maintains its majority only through a fragile coalition with several other political parties. Israel's political situation is fluid. There's a good chance that by the time you read this, it will have changed.

As you can imagine, the fluidity of Israel's political situation generates a bewildering array of viewpoints. In my visits to Israel, I've spent hours in conversations with people from left to right, from peace activists to military leaders. Given the diversity of viewpoints, the only reason anything happens is that Israelis seem bound together by a sense of destiny, common enemies, and geographical constraints. One may ignore people who reside on the other side of the world but not those with whom one shares a room. Israelis move forward through hard-won consensus between disagreeing parties. And move forward they do. As a Middle Eastern nation without well-developed oil or natural gas and surrounded by aggressive enemies, Israel has developed the fourth most successful economy among members of the Organization for Economic Cooperation and Development.[30] Despite the fierce individualism and perplexing array of viewpoints, Israel has forged the only democracy in the Middle East. It is the only nation in the region where women are equal to men and where people can live in freedom regardless of their religion, political beliefs, or sexual orientation. On the surface, it seems chaotic. But as a friend of mine on our trip commented, "They have a 'we' that I have not experienced in the United States."

Sometimes in history, that sense of "we" dissolved. In the Old Testament, the Jews experienced civil war, pitting two of Israel's tribes against the other ten. This split made it easier for their mutual enemies to prevail over them. Miraculously, Israel reconstituted for several hundred more years before Rome destroyed Jerusalem in AD 70. Even given Rome's military might, this was not inevitable. The historian Josephus noted that Jerusalem was fortified, armed, and supplied. Yet it fell because its leaders divided into three factions that sowed dissension, destroyed one another's food supplies, and attacked the civilian population. Instead of breaking the back of Roman domination, Jerusalem conquered itself. The rest of the world was left enslaved to Rome for another four hundred years. As Jonathan Sacks put it, "When Jews in the past had a sense of purpose, nothing could defeat them. When they lacked it, they found ingenious ways of almost defeating themselves."[31]

Today, Israelis also find themselves with a fragile internal peace even as tensions over Israel's existence threaten to escalate into a broad Middle Eastern war. People I spoke to on my recent trip are angry at their government for not protecting them against the October 7 attacks. They resent current leaders for relying on technology rather than ground troops to secure the border. They agonize about the present government's inability to rescue the hostages. Will all this frustration lead to a change in government and a new way of Israel relating to its neighbors? Only time will tell. Meanwhile, the terror campaign against it continues unabated.

> Israel is the only nation in the region where women are equal to men and where people can live in freedom regardless of their religion, political beliefs, or sexual orientation.

The Long-Running Terror Campaign That Explains Israel's Determination to Survive

Terrorism is the scourge of the world. The late French President Jacques Chirac said, "Terrorism has become the systematic weapon of war that knows no borders and seldom has a face." Terror groups have formed out of both extreme left and extreme right viewpoints and among most of the world's religions. But the bulk of terror attacks—85 percent of them—occur in Muslim countries.

Israel sits in the middle of this conflict, facing multiple threats just a few miles from its borders. Gaza is a warfront for Israel. Lebanon, Syria, and Iran are also warfronts, though Iran's capital is a long day's drive away, assuming you could get there. Intelligence Officer Itamar Ben David points out that even as Israel battles Hamas, it also faces forty thousand gunmen in the West Bank, one hundred thousand in Lebanon, and at least twenty thousand in Syria. Relations with Egypt, Israel's neighbor to the south, are always tense. In Jordan, with which Israel shares a four-hundred-mile border, people are mired in poverty; and the king's hold on power often seems tenuous. If any of these situations deteriorated to the point of war, Israel could be quickly overwhelmed.

> Nearly all of America's warfronts have been outside the American mainland. For Israel, any one of its fronts can be reached by car in less than two hours.

Aside from the ever-present threat of terrorism, the state of Israel has experienced full-scale wars several times in its short seventy-five years of existence: immediately after its founding in 1948, in 1967, and in 1973. Each of these constituted an existential threat. Israel has been on a war footing with Lebanon and with the Palestinian leadership for decades.

Americans have no context for this kind of threat. Aside from the British invasions around the time of its founding, the Civil War, and the 9/11 terrorist attacks, America's warfronts have been outside the American mainland. For Israel, any one of its fronts can be reached by car in a few hours.

It's important to put the October 7 Hamas attack in perspective. The twelve hundred killed that day would be equivalent to forty-two thousand Americans, or about fourteen times as many as were killed in the 9/11 terrorist attacks. Dr. Eric Patterson, a leading expert on Just War Theory, offers the following analogy: "I grew up in San Diego. If a criminal group came across the border from Tijuana and killed 42,000 men, women, and children in cold blood, raping women, and posting videos to YouTube accompanied by a Braveheart soundtrack, wouldn't we demand a reckoning?"[32]

But it's even worse than that. Israel's enemies attack it constantly. Since 1996, Israel has experienced 132 suicide bombings, claiming the lives of 770 people. It has endured thirty thousand rocket attacks (yes, you read that number correctly). The nation is so small that these rockets can reach their targets in less than a minute. Once the air raid sirens sound, Israelis have just seconds to take cover. Most Americans have no idea how it would be possible to survive and thrive in such a situation. This is what Israel has faced every day for seventy-five years.

On October 7, Israelis were startled awake by the sound of rockets and air-raid sirens. That's not unusual. But on that day, the rockets just kept coming. A thousand. Five thousand. Ultimately, fourteen thousand were launched at targets inside Israel. As they landed, three thousand terrorists armed with rifles, grenades, and RPGs rushed out of their Gaza enclave into Israeli settlements and commenced a horrifying slaughter. Their goal was not only to terrorize and kill people but also to destroy their very way of life. They ruined entire communities and decimated as much of Israel's infrastructure as they could, destroying up to 70 percent of Israel's agricultural production.[33] It will take years to recover.

> Hamas's goal was not only to terrorize and kill people but also to destroy their very way of life.

According to one military source I spoke with, a thousand of the Hamas fighters were trained. They led a thousand apprentice warriors eager to prove their loyalty to Allah. A thousand armed Gazans joined them to plunder their hated Jewish neighbors.

In a recent Q & A with Gen Z young adults, a perceptive student asked, "We know Hamas is bad. We feel sorry for the Israelis and all the Gazan non-combatants who have been caught up in the conflict. But why should Christians care about this conflict more than other conflicts that are happening in the world?"

There are 193 nations in the world. Many of them are in conflict. Why focus on Israel? It's a fair question. How would you answer it? My answer is what we'll talk about in the next chapter.

CHAPTER 4

The Israel of Your **Bible**

In 2022, more than half of Americans said they held favorable views of Israel.[34] Support is highest among older Americans and lowest among younger Americans. Young adults are almost twice as likely as older adults to view Israel unfavorably.[35] The highest levels of support for Israel are typically among evangelical Christians, but that is changing as well. As we saw in chapter two, young evangelicals' support of Israel has dropped in half since 2018.

The young adults I work with are asking tough questions: aside from loving Jews as neighbors, is it biblically required to be pro-Israel? Hasn't Christianity made Judaism irrelevant in God's plan? How does the modern state of Israel have anything to do with the Bible?

The Israel/Hamas war and the larger Israel/Palestine conflict are geographical battles over competing land claims. They are also spiritual

> The Israel/Palestine conflict is both a geographical battle over competing land claims and a spiritual battle over God's plan for the world.

battles over God's plan for the world.

While in Israel, our group conversed with Calev Myers, a partner in one of Israel's leading law firms and a civil rights activist who vigorously defends the rights of Palestinians against abuses by Hamas. We asked Calev, "What do you think is behind the left's open embrace of Hamas, which they know is a terrorist group that targets innocent men, women, and children?"

His reply was instant: "The only thing that explains the embrace of Hamas is a deep hatred of God and the Bible."

This was hard for me to accept. I'm not a student of end times prophecy. I'm leery of a lot of teachings I've heard on spiritual warfare. I don't like over-spiritualizing things. At the same time, though, I don't want to *under*-spiritualize them. In the decades I've spent studying a biblical worldview, I have met a lot of influential people who believe America would be better off if its Judeo-Christian foundation were replaced with some sort of utopian secular global government. Obviously, if this is their aim, they must first attack God. But I believe the existence of a people chosen by God is a constant reminder that there is a God and that He has a plan for the world.

Every anti-God movement from Haman in the Old Testament to the Bolsheviks to the Nazis all sought to destroy the Jewish people *because they are a people*, regardless of their level of religious practice. Secular Jews are as likely as religious Jews to be targeted. Relatedly, persecution of Christians is also soaring. The World Watch List says that around 365 million Christians around the world are subject to "high levels of persecution and discrimination" and that this number has grown by 10 percent in the last year.[36]

> I believe the existence of a people chosen by God is a constant reminder that there is a God and that He has a plan for the world.

The central question of this chapter, though, relates to the Jewish people. What does the Bible itself teach about the centrality of Israel and the Jews in God's plan?

Four Biblical Aspects of Israel and the Jewish People

From its first chapters to its last, the Bible forms an overarching narrative about life. The Jewish people play a central role in this narrative. Here are four aspects of that narrative relevant to this book:

1. **God is a God of history.** At the center of the Judeo-Christian worldview is a God *of* history who has revealed Himself *in* history. God created. Humans fell into sin. God made a way of redemption and is restoring all things. This work will continue until the end of time when God will make His dwelling with humanity (see Revelation 21). History isn't a random series of events. History is going somewhere, and it is going there on purpose.

2. **All human beings have value as image-bearers of God.** People and societies flourish through a high view of humanity based on the sovereignty of God. This one aspect of the Judeo-Christian worldview has provided greater political, religious, and economic freedom than any other foundational principle in human history. Communist, Nazi, and jihadist ideas, by contrast, always—*always*—lead to wreck and ruin. To stand against bad ideas, we have to de-center from the notion that we each have our "own truth." The scriptural challenge is to move from asking "What do *I* want" to "What does *God* want?"

   > People and societies flourish through a high view of humanity based on the sovereignty of God

3. **The earth—our physical bodies and our place in it—matters.** A third aspect of a Judeo-Christian worldview is that God works at specific times, in specific places, through specific people. God cares about our physical existence and the course of our lives. This core aspect of Scripture was challenged in the first and second centuries by Gnosticism. Gnosticism claimed a secret knowledge—*gnosis*—that our relationship with God is spiritual and has nothing to do with the physical world. It's about spirit, not body.[37] [38]

Doubtless, some early Christians found Gnosticism compelling because they themselves were refugees and under the constant threat of bodily persecution. But the early church fathers considered Gnosticism a heresy. The Apostles' Creed—which focused on God entering creation itself through Jesus—was devised as a line-by-line refutation of Gnostic claims. Today, Gnosticism is making a comeback among people who think that creation is irredeemably ruined and that our best hope is to focus on our spiritual selves as if we were disembodied creatures.

4. **God chose to work through the Jewish people to carry out His plan for the world.** Most Christians acknowledge that God worked through the Jews in the past. But there has been a long-running debate on whether Jews play a role in God's plan now that Christ has come. Some Christian theologians think that the spiritual importance of Christ replaced or fulfilled the physical importance of the Jews. This view is sometimes called supersessionism.

My Jewish friends are very sensitive about supersessionism. To them, the idea that Christianity replaced Judaism in God's plan gave rise to anti-Semitism, from the times of the Spanish Inquisition to twentieth-century Nazism. A few Christian theologians, recognizing this sensitivity, have moved away from using terms like supersessionism or replacement theology and embraced terms like "fulfillment theology" instead.[39] Regardless of the terms we use, we can all agree, the mistreatment of Jews as a people should never be supported. Our theology should never result in marginalizing anyone, let alone an entire people group.

The framework of Christian thought about the role of the Jews in God's plan was in place well before the establishment of the modern state of Israel in 1948. Before 1948, since Jews were dispersed throughout the world, the idea of "Israel" was sometimes seen by Christian theologians as more of a spiritual concept than a national identity. How ought the establishment of the modern state of Israel affect our theological reflection? I may not be a trained Bible scholar, but I respectfully hope that whatever views we hold, we can agree that the Bible teaches that God endowed the Jewish people with a special calling, which was to be a blessing to the nations, and that our own calling as Christians is related to, not separate from, that calling.

These four aspects of a biblical worldview—God is active in the world; humans bear God's image; our physical existence matters; and God worked through the Jews—bear strongly on how we view the situation in the Middle East.

Being a Blessing to the Nations

Saying that the Jewish people were chosen by God is not to say that they are better than other people groups, such as various Palestinian tribes. Palestinians and Jews both bear God's image, and it is wrong to say that Jews have more value. Rather, saying that the Jewish people were chosen by God is to acknowledge that they have played a central role in God's plan for the world. Jews have indeed brought blessing—including political, economic, and religious freedom—to the world. My view is that with all its flaws, the Jewish state of Israel at *this* time in *that* part of the world must be cultivated, not abandoned or destroyed.

> Saying that the Jewish people were chosen by God is to acknowledge that God has worked and does work through the Jewish people.

In chapter three, I shared about the blessing that ancient Israel was to the founding of the United States. America's founders studied Scripture as they formed a government and constitution. In fact, they quoted more from Scripture than all other sources put together. They weren't just picking and choosing Bible verses to support their opinions, as so many do today. Instead, they drew inspiration from the Hebrew republic as recorded in the Old Testament.[40] It was America's resulting constitutional framework that enabled the United States to move toward a "more perfect union," correcting its errors and pursuing greater justice.

Human fallenness, a doctrine the founders gleaned from Scripture, also factored into the kind of government they formed. As historian Wilfred M. McClay put it, they believed that the best constitution was one "built with the crooked timber of selfish humanity in mind."[41] That's why the founders formed three branches of government. They wanted each branch to check and balance the others to make it difficult for one person or group to take complete control.

America's debt to the Jews is just one example of the biblical principle of Jews being a blessing to the nations—that is, to all people, nations, tribes, and tongues. It all began in Genesis, where God said to Abram (later renamed Abraham by God), "I will make of you a great nation, and I will bless you and make your name great, so that you will be a blessing. I will bless those who bless you, and him who dishonors you I will curse, and in you all the families of the earth shall be blessed" (Genesis 12:1-3).

As South African Bible teacher Riaan Heyns put it in a conversation we had about Israel, God's covenant with Israel was *from* God, *through* Israel, *to* the nations. But how does this relate to Christians today?

The Story of God's Covenant

In Galatians 3:6-9, the apostle Paul affirmed that Abraham "believed God, and it was counted to him as righteousness." He then wrote, "So then, those who are of faith are *blessed along with* Abraham, the man of faith" (emphasis added).

Paul's understanding of Scripture was based on the idea of covenant. In the time of Abraham, covenants between people were sealed by the parties to the covenant passing between the divided halves of an animal carcass, in essence saying, "May what happened to this animal happen to me if I violate this covenant." In God's covenant with Abraham, recorded in Genesis 15, God alone passed between the pieces of flesh. We call it the Abrahamic covenant, but it wasn't technically *with* Abraham. It was God making a covenant with Himself *on behalf of* Abraham and his descendants. God put His own nature and reputation on the line as a covenantal guarantee. God is the One who decides whether this covenant still applies, whether it has been broken, how it can be renewed, or whether its obligations have been fulfilled.

For most of Christian history, the nation of Israel did not exist as a geographical entity, so some commentators naturally assumed that

> Christians don't replace Jews in God's plan; they join them.

"Israel" was a spiritual concept, not a physical one. The covenant language of Scripture, however, is related to the land. The Abrahamic covenant was about the people *in the land*. God promised to bring His people into the land (Exodus 6:7-8). God swore to give the land as an inheritance (Deuteronomy 30:20). Ezekiel 36:28 says, "You shall dwell in the land that I gave to your fathers." Deuteronomy 11:12 says, "The eyes of the Lord your God are always upon it, from the beginning of the year to the end of the year." Psalm 105:8-11 says, "He remembers his covenant forever, the word that he commanded, for a thousand generations, the covenant that he made with Abraham, his sworn promise to Isaac, which he confirmed to Jacob as a statute, to Israel as an everlasting covenant, saying, 'To you I will give the land of Canaan as your portion for an inheritance.'"

As I see it, viewing "Israel" only as a spiritual metaphor diminishes the significance of Israel as an actual, physical, geographical concern. Is this what the New Testament teaches? Many think so. They interpret the apostle Paul's irritation at some Jews' resistance to Christ's gospel as intended to subvert the spiritual entity of Judaism and elevate the spiritual entity of the "Church."

Now, I'm reasonably certain that you didn't pick up this book because you were eager to go down theological rabbit holes. Perhaps we don't need to. At face value, we can see that Paul hated it when the Jews he was writing about felt superior because they were God's original chosen people. He also hated it when Gentiles claimed superiority at being "above" the Jews' complicated religious laws. Paul's writings go to great lengths to reconcile the two groups. His message is "God is the One who saves, so be humble." As a friend of mine puts it, humility is a gateway to understanding revelation.

Paul wrote in Romans 1:16 that the power of God for salvation came "to the Jew first and also to the Greek." In Romans 11, he explained that the Gentiles had been grafted *into* God's tree. He repeatedly emphasized that God is not done with the Jews. In fact, in verse twenty-nine, he wrote that "the gifts and the calling of God are irrevocable."

What should Christians make of this? Here's my suggestion. Let's spend more time marveling at the wonder of Gentiles being grafted *into* God's tree and less time speculating about whether some or all Jews were grafted *out*.

My renewed fascination with God's extraordinary plan for the world has given me a new respect for the Jewish roots of my faith. I've started to study the New Testament in *light* of the Old Testament as one grand narrative. This has helped me understand some of the Bible's baffling teachings a little bit better, such as with prophecies recorded in Daniel, Isaiah, Jeremiah, and Ezekiel.

In Matthew 25:31, for example, Jesus prophesies about Himself, saying, "'When the Son of Man comes in his glory, and all the angels with him, then he will sit on his glorious throne.'" This is a direct reference to Old Testament prophecies, such as Isaiah 9:7—"Of the increase of his government and of peace there will be no end, on the throne of David and over his kingdom"—and Zechariah 14:9—"And the Lord will be king over all the earth. On that day the Lord will be one and his name one."

Even the prophetic language used by the apostle John in the book of Revelation draws on Old Testament prophecies, such as Isaiah 52, 54, and 60. John writes that at the end of all things, "He will wipe away every tear from their eyes, and death shall be no more, neither shall there be mourning, nor crying, nor pain anymore, for the former things have passed away" (Revelation 21:4). This ties back to Isaiah 25:8, which says, "He will swallow up death forever; and the Lord God will wipe away tears from all faces, and the reproach of his people he will take away from all the earth, for the Lord has spoken."

> The Jewish origins of the work of Christ were obvious to the apostles. Jesus was a Jew. He is a Jew. He died and rose again as a Jew and is returning as a Jew.

The prophet Ezekiel describes the Holy City in detail. It is the new Jerusalem. Living waters will flow out of it (Zechariah 14:6-8). Some of the descriptions of the new Jerusalem in Revelation harken back to the non-canonical book of Tobit, which is not in most Protestant Bibles but is familiar to those of a Catholic, Orthodox, or Anglican tradition. Tobit describes the new Jerusalem in detail, including the construction of its gates, walls, towers, and streets (see Tobit 13:16-17). The Jewish origins of the work of Christ seemed readily apparent to the apostles. Jesus was a Jew. He *is* a Jew. He died and rose again as a Jew and is returning as a Jew.

How God's Covenant Applies to Jews and Christians

The ties between the Old Testament and the New Testament help us recognize the continuous nature of God's plan in the past, in the present, and in the future. It describes a *consummation* of God's covenant with the Jews, not an alternate reality apart from it. The apostle Peter is explicit about this in 1 Peter 1:10-12: "Concerning this salvation, prophets who prophesied about the grace that was to be yours searched and investigated it, investigating the time and circumstances that the Spirit of Christ within them indicated when it testified in advance to the sufferings destined for Christ and the glories to follow them. *It was revealed to them that they were serving not themselves but you*" (emphasis added).

> The New Testament is not describing an alternate reality apart from God's covenant with the Jews. It is describing the consummation of that covenant.

The prophets of old knew they worked in the service of God's grand plan to fashion for Himself a people from all nations of the earth. So is it possible that the modern state of Israel bears no relationship to the ancient Israel established by God? Maybe. But Scripture seems to indicate that God has an overarching plan for history, and this his plan flowed through the Jewish people in the land. Some of the Bible's prophecies have been fulfilled. Others are being fulfilled. We anticipate the fulfillment of yet others in the future. Either way, I am persuaded that today's Israel is part of a continuous plan of God that has involved the Jews for more than three thousand years.

Modern Israel reflects this history. It is a Jewish state and a homeland for the Jewish people. Most of its citizens are Jews. Israel's Basic Law (its constitution-like agreement) is based on the book of Deuteronomy. Its national holidays are Jewish holidays originating in Bible times. It incorporates Hebrew law into everything from marriages being performed by rabbis to the kosher food served at government installations. Israel's flag is designed based on a Jewish prayer shawl.

To be clear, acknowledging the special place of the Jews is not to say that there is no place for secular people or Muslims or any other religious group in Israel. Religious diversity is welcomed in Israel, including the religion of non-belief. But just as Indians are from India and Egyptians are from Egypt, Jews are from Judea. This has been the case for over three thousand years.

Those who claim that God doesn't care about present-day Israel any more than any other nation are certainly entitled to their opinion. But I'm encouraging Christians to take a larger view of God's working through time, the nature of God's covenant, the cultural realities reflected in the Bible, the relationship between the people and the land, and the actual words of Scripture. The gospel of Jesus is not somehow outside of or above physical reality, as the Gnostics taught. In the past, "Israel" may have been viewed as a non-physical, spiritual concept. I see the reestablishment of the state of Israel in 1948 as changing that paradigm, both geopolitically and theopolitically.

> Just as Indians are from India and Egyptians are from Egypt, Jews are from Judea. This has been the case for over three thousand years.

Jews have a physical presence in the land of their history. Whether you agree with how it happened or how they are stewarding it, this is the reality. It is also a reality that Israel is under attack from every quarter in a battle between competing worldviews. The history of Palestine, the religion of Islam, and the aims of the apocalyptic rape-and-death cult called Hamas all figure in a larger struggle for truth. This is what we urgently need to understand.

PART 2

ISRAEL AND THE **BATTLE** OF WORLDVIEWS

CHAPTER 5

Generation
Indoctrination

After October 7, the world's reaction to the Hamas attacks and Israel's blistering military response fell along predictable lines. It quickly became clear that this is not your parents' Israel/Palestine conflict. The very existence of Hamas unalterably disrupts the standard narrative for understanding the Middle East.

In the last thirty years, Hamas has brutally inserted itself into the unstable and uneasy truce between Israel and other nations of the world and between Islam and Judaism. Through cycles of violence, appeals to pity, and more violence, it has shamelessly appropriated the world's goodwill toward beleaguered Palestinians and wrested the prophet's mantle from the Ummah, the

> The very existence of Hamas unalterably disrupts the standard narrative for understanding the Middle East.

global Islamic community. Its public pronouncements have drawn a line in the sand: *either embrace our vision for an Islamist-dominated Palestine in which Israel is snuffed out, or you are against the prophet himself.*

So far, most of the world's Muslim nations have declined to join Hamas in their self-described campaign of "resistance." These nations sympathize with the Palestinians, surely, but that doesn't mean they want them arriving on their own shores. No Arab nations other than Jordan have ever offered citizenship to the Palestinians, and none are offering it now. Syria once offered Hamas refuge but kicked it out after it sparked a civil war. Not even the bad guys want to have anything to do with Hamas—except for Iran, which sees it as a handy tool to pry Israel out of the world community. But Hamas does have fellow travelers. Many of them are in America, operating under the protection of universities across the land.

The American Left: Hamas's Dupes

Ironically, aside from Iran, the most favorable response to Hamas's radical Islamist vision and hatred of the Jews has been from the progressive left, centered largely in institutions of higher education. Here, decades of anti-American, postmodernist instruction have cultivated a moist environment in which the viruses of radical ideology fester. Its petri dish carries the label "social justice"; but below its visible surface, proto-Marxist viruses multiply. The world is simple, it says. It is the oppressors versus the oppressed. Those judged by the academic elite to be oppressed may justly use any tactics at their disposal to overthrow their oppressors.

Hamas, for its part, happily interprets the progressive left's obeisance as evidence of its own rightness. It draws energy from Jew-hatred and anti-Israel propaganda. It knows that a world in which Jews are threatened as seriously as in the days leading up to the Holocaust is a world in which it might achieve its aims. Hamas has duped the progressive left. But it is also mistaken about the progressive left's real interests. The long-running feud between the state of Israel and the two dominant Palestinian tribes was never just a battle over a tiny sliver of land in the Middle East. It was never *just* about Israel's right to self-determination and the plight of Palestinians. It is about diminishing the influence of the Judeo-Christian worldview, the free market system, and representative government. It is a battle over the future of Western civilization.

The progressive left's reflex response to October 7 reveals this. Given the wrenching evidence of Hamas's crimes against innocent Israelis, you might expect some deep soul-searching on the part of those advocating for social justice—perhaps candlelight vigils for the victims and the hostages or Gentiles reaching out to Jewish neighbors to offer comfort. You might expect calls for Hamas to be dismantled based on its many crimes against the Palestinian people in Gaza. You would be wrong.

Just two days after the October 7 massacre, 127 university-based chapters of a group called Students for Justice in Palestine (SJP) released a statement saying that Hamas's genocidal attacks were justified and blaming *Israel* for committing genocide.[42] SJP released this statement almost a full week before Israel ramped up its counter-offensive in Gaza, while the IDF was still rooting out terrorists from the homes of their victims and Israelis were enduring Hezbollah missile attacks from the north.

> The long-running feud between the state of Israel and the Palestinian people was never just a battle over a tiny sliver of land in the Middle East. It's a battle over the future of Western civilization.

In retrospect, it seems obvious that Hamas's propaganda campaign had been planned alongside the military one. But Hamas lackeys on US campuses apparently didn't get the memo about waiting until Israel responded militarily before condemning it for responding militarily. Imagine SJP's surprise when wealthy, progressive donors—not just conservative ones—called them out. Congressional hearings followed. Two high-profile college presidents lost their jobs. The rest hired expensive PR firms to convince the world that it had misheard what they had said and that, in any event, what they said was not what they meant. Still, what caught most people—including myself—off guard was the vast cultural divide the conflict exposed.

Oppressor Versus Oppressed Narrative

To be sure, the narrative line favoring the Palestinian cause, with Hamas at its center, is a straight one: Israel is richer; Gaza is poorer. Israel's military is well-trained and well-equipped; Hamas is poorly trained by comparison and fighting with leftover Iranian weapons smuggled through Egypt. Hamas has killed its thousands, Israel its tens of thousands. In the minds of many, any blow Hamas strikes against Israel is a blow *for* all Palestinians. As Linda Sarsour, leader of the Women's March put it, Palestine is "the social justice cause of our generation."

To be fair, it isn't just progressive leftists who embrace this narrative. A growing number of self-identified Christians reason that since the Gazans are suffering more, they must be more righteous. Israel is absolutely more powerful, they say, and absolute power corrupts absolutely. The level of support for Israel among Gen Z evangelicals has dropped in half since 2018, according to the Brookings Institution.[43]

> Obviously, being against Israel's policies doesn't mean that one is by default pro-terrorism. But groups like Hamas are the greatest beneficiaries of the oppressor/oppressed mindset.

Many libertarian-leaning Gen Zers are also unmoved by America's history of supporting Israel. It's not that they support Hamas but that they see Israel as a millstone around President Biden's neck. They revel in Biden's sinking poll numbers in battleground states and attribute this to his support of Israel, however uneven it may be. Also, they're wary of repeating the expensive and largely fruitless military entanglements that mired American in foreign wars for two decades after 9/11, at a cost of $8 trillion, millions dead, and tens of millions displaced. Annual debt payments of hundreds of billions of dollars will fall on the shoulders of the rising generation, and they're understandably irate. Their "America first" mindset is quickly morphing into an "America only" one, at least as far as military involvement is concerned.[44]

How Do You Find Truth in the Noise?

Obviously, being against Israel's policies doesn't mean that one is by default pro-terrorism. But it is naïve to think that groups like Hamas are not the greatest beneficiaries of the oppressor/oppressed mindset. It is also naïve to think that this will somehow not translate into attacks against the United States, as Hamas has called for.[45]

I began my exploration asking, "How did an entire generation get suckered by Hamas, which is clearly an apocalyptic rape-and-death cult?" But my search for answers quickly led to deeper questions. How are we to understand the battle of worldviews playing out over Israel and the Palestinian people? Is Israel's counter-offensive against Hamas a just one, or is it genocide? Only when we get clarity about these issues can we turn our attention to how to rescue a generation from false ideologies—a question that goes far beyond Middle East conflict.

Where is the truth in the noise? Reading the Western press regarding Israel feels a little like reading German newspaper accounts during the Second World War. Even if the facts line up, the narrative is written in a way that obscures their true meaning. Finding good insight from a biblical worldview is equally difficult. Beyond speculation about end-times prophecy and the "America, good—Israel, good" cheerleading, how are we to understand what is really happening in the Middle East from a biblical worldview?

What we dare not do is shrug off the current conflict as an intractable war about which we can do nothing. A friend recently pointed out a convicting passage from C. S. Lewis' *Screwtape Letters* in which the demon Screwtape advises his protégé about how to advance the cause of evil in the mind and heart of his target. The key, says Screwtape, is not to dull his feelings but to keep him from *acting* on his feelings: "The more often he feels without acting, the less he will be able ever to act, and, in the long run, the less he will be able to feel."[46] Much about the Israel/Palestine conflict is hard to understand. But that does not mean it can't be understood.

> What we dare not do is shrug off the current conflict as an intractable war about which we can do nothing.

As Rachel Goldberg, the mother of an October 7 hostage, reminded a group of us in Jerusalem, "Hard is not bad. Hard is just hard."

The goal of a biblical worldview is not to make hard things easier but to make foggy things clearer. So let's get started by examining the war of worldviews that lies below the surface of today's most perplexing problems.

CHAPTER 6

Warring
Worldviews

Anti-Semitism is rising once again. This time it isn't rooted in dark hovels where shifty neo-Nazis plan the rebirth of fascism. It is, rather, carried along by a stubborn double standard that itself stems from the postmodern turn in higher education.

In 2021, three respected researchers conducted an eye-opening study of where this new kind of anti-Semitism—the double-standard that denies the fundamental legitimacy of Judaism and of Israel—draws its energy. They found that not only does higher education not protect against anti-Semitism, but it also licenses it in a sophisticated, socially acceptable way. Those with advanced degrees were between 15 percent and 36 percent more unfavorable toward Jews and Israel when examples of certain social behaviors were about Jews rather than Black Lives

Matter (BLM) advocates or Muslims, and about Israel rather than other nations, such as Mexico.[47]

How Smart People Become Dupes

Certainly, education is imperative for a healthy society. But it does not follow that having more education inoculates people against evil ideas. It may even make some more susceptible. Nazism, for example, was largely an academic movement. According to Holocaust scholar Mark Roseman, half the Nazi leaders who planned the extermination of Europe's eleven million Jews carried the title "doctor."[48]

Education makes people vulnerable when it becomes a means of transmitting false ideologies. Marxism was an intellectual movement at first. It was carried along by coifed professors in ivory towers long before it infected self-styled revolutionaries in plundered palaces. Who could have imagined that a worldview birthed in a library by the bearded eccentric Karl Marx would have become such a totalizing and crushing force? Surely, Marx is one of those who rules the world from the grave.[49]

We ought to know better by now. One of the reasons we don't was explained by Joseph P. Overton from the Mackinac Center for Public Policy. Overton said that on any given issue, the range of "acceptable" ideas falls within a window. Picture a movie director framing a shot with her fingers. The audience doesn't see everything the director sees but only what the director *wants* them to see.

> Certainly, education is imperative for a healthy society. But it does not follow that having more education inoculates people against evil ideas.

The Overton Window explains why so many bright people at prestigious institutions can look at a world of truth and see it falsely. Buoyed by utopian schemes of remaking the world, reality with a capital "R" simply isn't within the window of the ideas they find thinkable. "It's the first effect of not believing in God that you lose your common sense and can't see things as they are," wrote G. K. Chesterton in his short story, "The Oracle of the Dog."[50] This is the painful lesson of the twentieth century. It took decades for the world to rouse itself from slumber and grudgingly admit the evils of Nazism and communism. Yet the core ideologies behind both—that everything in the world can be explained by an oppressor versus oppressed framework and that personal violence is called for if the offense is sufficiently great—remain lodged in the body politic. When new conflicts arise, they flare up anew.

> We humans flee the consequences of mind viruses, only to realize that we are their carriers. The more we try to escape, the more we spread the misery.

We humans flee the consequences of mind viruses, only to realize that we are their carriers. The more we try to escape, the more we spread the misery. I've invested the last decade studying the effects of mind viruses on the rising generation. My goal is to see generations of Christians restored to a healthy biblical worldview. This starts with God. In the search for truth, only God is truly objective. We will not know truth exhaustively, but this does not mean that we cannot know it truly. As journalist Marvin Olasky puts it, "Our hope relies on filling our fallen minds with God's vision."[51]

Discovering truth involves asking, at every moment, "God, what are You seeing that You want us to see? What are You hearing that You want us to hear? Where is Your attention directed that You want us to go?" Rediscovering a biblical worldview as a means of finding truth does not mean that we must baptize the actions of all those who claim to adhere to it. It means grounding our understanding of reality in the light of a transcendent metanarrative based on *hope* and *redemption*, not *hate* and *retribution*.

> Rediscovering a biblical worldview means grounding our understanding of reality in the light of a transcendent metanarrative based on *hope* and *redemption*, not *hate* and *retribution*.

We humans suffer from an astigmatism that makes clear vision frustratingly difficult to obtain. We see, as poet Matthew Arnold put it, "as on a darkling plain, swept by confused alarms of struggle and flight."[52] To even begin glimpsing the truth, we must confess our susceptibility to patterns of false ideas and, as best as we can, be honest about our culturally conditioned assumptions and preferred outcomes. We take false ideas captive (2 Corinthians 10:5). We must not be taken captive by them (Colossians 2:8).

Understanding Today's Dominating Worldviews

Today's mind viruses don't attack randomly. They fall into understandable patterns. Here are five such patterns of our time:

1. **Secularism—life is about** *control. Secular* comes from a Latin word meaning "lifespan." Secularism says that what matters is what happens during our lifetime. We have no transcendent guidance about solving the problems we face. The secularist perspective says that the brightest among us must direct the rest of us to ensure outcomes that the "brights" deem acceptable.

2. **Marxism—life is about** *capital.* Marxism says that only the material world exists. If this is true, human possibility is always constrained by scarcity. Inequality exists because some people have acquired, by theft, more than their fair share. Thirty-three times in the *Communist Manifesto*, Karl Marx called for abolishing the social structures that he blamed for this inequality—primarily the government, the economy, religion, and the family. All must be overthrown.[53]

3. **Postmodernism—life is about** *context.* According to this worldview, which was birthed out of Marxism, all of life must be viewed through the lens of power. Two kinds of people exist: oppressors and the oppressed. Those classed by academic elites as oppressors are, by definition, corrupt. They must be shamed and marginalized. After all, are they not the ones seeking to shame and marginalize the rest of us? Their "facts" are nothing more than a bid for power; their "truth" is an illusion.

4. **New spirituality—life is about** *consciousness.* A new spiritualist worldview says that at the core of reality is a higher consciousness, a force some people call "god." Everything is spiritual. Material reality doesn't really exist in the way we think of it. The sooner we realize this, the sooner we will feel at one with the universe and the sooner humanity can move toward perfection.[54]

5. **Islam—life is about** *conquering.* A sixth-century nomad named Muhammad claimed an angel revealed to him the sin of polytheism

and demanded that humanity unite around the worship of one God—*Allah*, in Arabic. Islam teaches that we all are born Muslim ("those who submit"). Disobedience must be conquered through jihad, through which humans cease their rebellion and resubmit to God in the way the Quran prescribes.

False Worldviews Take People Captive

Each of these five worldviews offers an assessment of our natural state, speculation about why humans are broken, and a plan of salvation. In each case, it's a collective salvation. The needs of the individual must be subsumed by the interests of the collective. If anyone opts out, it threatens the fate of the rest.

> We must fight for a coherent truth if we are to have any hope of waging a coherent fight for justice.

The Judeo-Christian worldview, by contrast, puts the needs and aspirations of the individual front and center. People have souls. They flourish in an environment that permits wide latitude for each person to decide what that flourishing will look like. The Judeo-Christian worldview believes in government by the consent of the governed. This makes it a threat to the utopian visions of the rest.

False worldviews rarely come into our minds fully formed. Bits and pieces of each hijack our already-compromised mental immune systems. We must fight for a coherent truth if we are to have any hope of waging a coherent fight for justice. Believers ought to understand the times as the men of Issachar did (1 Chronicles 12:32). If we don't understand what God wants us to see, how will we ever be able to do what God wants us to do?

Those who operate by God's Word and His Spirit ought to be known for their discernment. We do not presume that we speak *for* God, but our words and actions ought to at least speak well *of* Him. To understand what happened on October 7 from a biblical worldview, we must understand the history of the Palestinian conflict, the history of Hamas, and the relationship of both to the religion of Islam.

CHAPTER 7

Palestine and the Rise of Islam

Until the 1930s, the term "Palestinian" referred to Jews, Muslims, and Christians living in the historic land of Israel that had been named Palestine by Hadrian, following the destruction of Jerusalem and its temple in 70 AD.

Prior to the Second World War, the Grand Mufti of Jerusalem, Haj Amin al-Hussein, led an extreme Arab separatist movement. He went so far as to meet with Adolf Hitler to conspire about ridding the Middle East of Jews. In 1947, the United Nations developed a partition plan for the region designating two separate states, one Arab and one Jewish. The leaders of the Arab faction rejected this plan, as well as subsequent two-state solution plans

> Until the 1930s, the term "Palestinian" referred to Jews, Muslims, and Christians living in the historic land of Israel.

in 1967, 2000, and 2008. In 1964, Yassar Arafat formed the Palestinian Liberation Organization (PLO). It was Arafat who insisted that the term "Palestinian" be used to refer only to Arabs. The world has largely gone along with this distinction.

In 1967, as the result of a war between Israel and an alliance of Syria, Jordan, and Egypt, Israeli forces conquered and occupied significant sections of territory controlled by those nations. Most of this land was given back through various agreements in which Israel was promised peace in exchange for land. However, two Palestinian territories remain: the West Bank and Gaza. The West Bank refers to the west bank of the Jordan river, traditionally called Judea and Samaria. Of the three million residents of the West Bank, about half a million are Jews.

The West Bank is semi-autonomous, having gained this status through negotiations in which Israel gave back territory it had acquired when it fought back against Palestinian attacks in 1967. The West Bank is divided into three sections with overlapping governance by the Palestinian Authority (the governing body established by Arafat's PLO) and the Israeli military. The term "Israeli occupation" mainly refers to the application of Israeli military law in these three sections in various ways, including policing and checkpoints. The IDF does not reveal how many soldiers it has inside the West Bank, but it is probably about six thousand. An American city with a similar population (three million) would typically have a police force of nine thousand. Why is this called an "occupation" rather than "policing"? There may be many reasons, but one of them surely is that Palestinians resent the Jewish presence and the term "occupation" offers them a rhetorical advantage in denying Israel's legitimacy.

Where Is Gaza, and What Is It Like?

Of the two Palestinian territories, Gaza is far smaller. It is a "strip" of land boasting twenty-five miles of undeveloped Mediterranean coastline that is about seven miles across at its widest point. From 1967 to 2005, Israel's military had a presence there.

In 2005, as part of a peace agreement, Israel evicted Gaza's Jewish residents, bulldozed their homes, and withdrew its military presence. The territory was quickly taken over by Hamas—first through an election

(2006) and then a coup (2007) in which Hamas murdered or exiled the leaders of the opposing Fatah party. No elections have been held in Gaza since that time. In the most recent Israel/Hamas war, Israel's stated policy was to eliminate Hamas as a military and governing concern in Gaza. Although Israel pulled its troops out of Gaza in 2005, the security threats to Israel's existence by Hamas led it to inspect all shipments into Gaza by land or sea and deny entry for military equipment or equipment that Israel judged could be used for military purposes.

The situation is complicated further by the fact that the PLO in the West Bank and Hamas in Gaza, while both Muslim, are essentially at war with one another. According to the Israeli Arab journalist Khaled Abu Toameh, they hate each other more than they hate Israel. A "two-state solution" in which Palestine becomes its own country like Israel has been consistently rejected by the PLO. The rise of Hamas makes this rejection more likely to remain perma-

> According to the Israeli Arab journalist Khaled Abu Toameh, the PLO and Hamas hate each other more than they hate Israel.

nent because Hamas will settle for nothing short of Israel's annihilation, and the PLO appears to fear the rise of Hamas more than it despises the presence of the Israeli army in the West Bank.

In the next chapter, we'll look at the rise of Hamas in more detail. For now, it is sufficient to say that life in Gaza is much harder on its 2.5 million residents than life in the West Bank is for its three million residents or in Israel with its nine million. It was hard before the recent war and has gotten unimaginably harder since Hamas's October 7 attack.

Before the 2023 Israel/Hamas war, Gaza was relatively poor by the world's standards, but not desperately so. Its average wage was about $5,000 a year. This is much lower than Israel but higher than 140 other countries in the world, including Egypt, Iran, Turkey, Jordan, or even the Ukraine.[55] Charts of gross domestic product show that since Hamas took over Gaza, people have become significantly poorer. Their situation after October 7 is now even more miserable, and there are some signs that Gazans blame Hamas as much as they blame Israel. When we look at Hamas in more detail later, it will become obvious why this is the case.

Ninety-nine percent of Gazans are Muslim. No Jews live in Gaza. Fewer than a thousand Christians remain, despite regular persecution.

To understand the Palestinian issue, we must understand the basics of Islam and the divisions within the faith that give rise to groups like Hamas.

Islam—a Misunderstood Worldview

Islam means "submission." A Muslim is "one who submits" to Allah. Today Islam is a major world religion, boasting a membership of nearly one-fourth of the world's population. Islam is a worldview as nuanced as Christianity, Judaism, Buddhism, or Hinduism. It consists of a bewildering array of factions and different levels of convictions, interpretations, and commitments.

> Islam means "submission." A Muslim is "one who submits" to Allah.

Those who do not closely follow events in the Middle East assume that being Muslim and being Arab are the same thing. It's not true. Yes, most Arabs are Muslim, but most Muslims around the world are not Arabs. The largest Muslim populations in the world reside in Indonesia, followed by Pakistan, India, and Bangladesh. Nearly half of the world's Muslim population lives in these four countries.

The principles of Islam are embodied in *ummah*, the worldwide community of Muslims. Remember this term when we talk about the culture and doctrine of Hamas. Ummah is a strong force for Muslims. It binds them together through cultural practices, as well as religious identity. It provides a comforting sense of belonging and a reassuring hierarchy in which community leaders have a very high status and individual identity and interests give way to those of the community.[56] Ummah, though not a formal structure, exerts enormous power; it is something Muslims do not want to upset. To break away from it is to be alienated and lost.

Most Muslims in the world simply want to be free to engage in Muslim practice and traditions. Many Muslim nations are "moderate"—not in the sense of being less devout but in their eagerness to build economic ties with Western nations rather than bring about their destruction.[57]

Islam has two main sects, Shia and Sunni. Shiites believe that the leader of Islam must be descended from the prophet Muhammed's family. Such a man would be able to rule with perfect religious and political authority. Shiites hold a mystical belief in the return of Muhammad al-Madhi, the twelfth imam, who will secure Islam's global dominance.

Since the resurgence of strict Shia doctrines during the reign of Ayatollah Khomeni in 1979, Iran's leaders have seen Israel as a cancer whose very existence threatens the fulfilment of this vision.

Sunnis reject the idea that rulers must be direct descendants of Muhammed. They rely instead on a complex interplay of scholarly Quranic interpretation and political pragmatism to guide the nations they control.

Iran is Shiite. Its leaders control a Shiite army of one hundred thousand fighters in Lebanon, to Israel's north. Although very few of Gaza's residents are Shia, Iran allies with Hamas because of their mutual interest in the destruction of Israel.

In both the Shia and Sunni communities, a small but influential percentage of Muslims dream of establishing a global Islamic state and are willing to use violence to achieve this end. These radicals are hard to identify. They are not more likely to attend religious services. Often, they earn more money and stay in school longer. They are as likely as moderate Muslims to admire democracy, technology, and financial success.[58] The key difference between moderate and radical Muslims is that radicals are more likely to believe that the West "threatens and attempts to control their way of life"[59]

Many scholars are uncomfortable with "moderate" and "radical" as terms to distinguish groups of Muslims. To call

> Muslims are people who have grown up in or converted to Islam and just want to go about their lives. Islamists, on the other hand, believe that Shari'ah Law should trump all other laws.

someone a "moderate" implies that they are not serious about their faith. This is a distinction that many Muslims understandably reject. Perhaps it is helpful to refer instead to "Muslims" and "Islamists."[60] *Muslims* are people who have grown up in or converted to Islam, who are content to go about their lives as everyone else does.

Islamists, on the other hand, believe that Shari'ah law, the moral code of Islam outlined in the Quran and other historical teachings and rulings, should trump all other laws.[61] Diet, sexual practices, and the punishment of crime are all covered by Shari'ah law. Many of its provisions seem shockingly harsh to the Western mind, including slavery, wife beating, heavy taxation of Christians and Jews living in Muslim lands, and the killing of Muslims who convert to another faith.[62] [63]

Most importantly, Muslims and Islamists differ in their understanding of jihad. In Islam, everyone who has ever been born in the world was born in submission to Allah. That is, everyone starts out as Muslim. Those who are not now Muslim are in rebellion against Allah. Jihad means to fight against this rebellion. It is clearly commanded in the Quran of all Muslims.[64]

Since jihad is required of all Muslims and always described in a warlike fashion in Islamic writings, the Muslim community faces a perplexing dilemma. Muslims and Islamists deal with this dilemma in dramatically different ways. Most Muslims think of jihad—if they think about it at all—as a form of personal self-discipline that has nothing to do with warfare.[65] Islamists, on the other hand, see jihad as the conquest of non-believing nations.[66] Islamists include as legitimate "defense" anything that defeats resistance to Islam. Peace will only occur when non-believers submit.[67]

> Among Islamists are many who believe physical violence is permitted as a tool to destroy the influence of the rebellious Western world. Hamas is firmly in this camp.

Among Islamists are many who have weaponized their beliefs. They believe physical violence is permitted as a tool to destroy the influence of the rebellious Jews or even the larger Western world.[68] Hamas is firmly in this camp. Nothing—not even the well-being of the Gazans it rules—must be allowed to stand in the way of removing the stain of humiliation that Israel's existence represents.

Obviously, such a short discussion cannot do justice to a worldview that has existed and developed for more than fourteen hundred years. But as we will see, the distinction between Muslim and Islamist will help explain what the Hamas terrorist group is all about and how it holds Palestinians hostage and threatens Israel.

CHAPTER 8

Hamas—Inside an Apocalyptic Rape-and-Death Cult

"Hamas," is an Arabic acronym for Islamic Resistance Movement. It was founded in the late 1980s by Sheikh Ahmed Yassin, a Palestinian cleric who got involved with Egypt's Muslim Brotherhood while studying Islam in Cairo. In 1997, the United States designated Hamas a foreign terrorist organization.

Hamas made a bad situation in Gaza even worse. The early 2000s could have been a positive turning point for the territory. The Israeli military and Jewish residents were gone. Hamas completely controlled the territory politically and militarily. It had the patronage of two oil-rich nations and the goodwill of most of the world. A peace plan was on the table for a two-state solution. Israel had agreed to it. Foreign aid poured into Gaza to the tune of $35 billion, fifteen times as much money as the Marshall Plan that reconstructed Europe after the Second World War.

> Hamas made a bad situation in Gaza even worse. Its primary commitment—far above all other interests—was and is to eliminate the state of Israel.

Hamas had a choice: attempt peaceful relations with Israel and turn its twenty-five miles of Mediterranean coastline into a prosperous trading post like Dubai or buy weapons, build tunnels, and prepare for war. It chose the latter course, not because it was advantageous to the Gazans but because Hamas's primary commitment—far above all other interests—was and is to eliminate the state of Israel.

What Hamas Believes

In its short history, at its founding and again in 2017, Hamas released a charter outlining its vision and mission. The original document, quoting the Quran, explicitly called for the killing of Jews. The 2017 "Document of General Principles and Policies" removed some of the extreme language about killing Jews while retaining the same aims of placing itself at the center of concern for the global Islamic community (Ummah) and eliminating the "Zionist project," Israel.

Here are some direct quotes from the 2017 charter that outline Hamas's aims:

- **Become the focal point of Islam:** "Palestine is the spirit of the Ummah and its central cause."[69] "Islam—for Hamas—provides a comprehensive way of life and an order that is fit for purpose at all times and in all places."[70] "The Zionist project does not target the Palestinian people alone; it is the enemy of the Arab and Islamic Ummah posing a grave threat to its security and interests."[71]

- **Eliminate Israel:** "Hamas believes that no part of the land of Palestine shall be compromised or conceded, irrespective of the causes, the circumstances and the pressures and no matter how long the occupation lasts."[72] "Not one stone of Jerusalem can be surrendered or relinquished."[73]

- **Assert the right to commit acts of violence:** "Resistance and jihad for the liberation of Palestine will remain a legitimate right, a duty and an honour for all the sons and daughters of our people and our Ummah."[74] "Resisting the occupation with all means and methods is a legitimate right guaranteed by divine laws and by international norms and laws."[75]

To summarize, Hamas claims to be based on Islamic beliefs and insists that Palestine is the "central cause" of the global community of Islam. The "Zionist project"—Israel—must be abolished. Hamas considers anything that achieves this goal as legitimate self-defense.

How Hamas Justifies October 7

After the October 7 attacks, which Hamas called Operation Al-Aqsa Flood, Hamas released a sixteen-page document entitled, "Our Narrative." It's an odd phrasing. Imagine going to court and telling the judge, "Let me offer my narrative." Surely, the judge would reply, "How about if you just tell the truth?" But to a terrorist organization such as Hamas, truth is what serves the interests of its leaders. Lies that support the interests of Hamas are, by definition, the truth. Peace can be achieved only by the elimination of the "Zionist entity."

> Hamas considers anything that leads to the abolition of the "Zionist project"—Israel— as legitimate self-defense.

In its narrative, Hamas claims that October 7 was a necessary step to confront all Israeli conspiracies against the Palestinian people and their cause. It was a defensive act designed to end Israel's occupation—not of the Palestinian territories but of *all* the land that Hamas thinks should never have been given to Israel in the first place.[76]

Hamas claimed that "the Palestinian resistance was fully disciplined and committed to the Islamic values during the operation and that the Palestinian fighters only targeted the occupation soldiers and those who carried weapons against our people" and that "the Palestinian fighters were keen to avoid harming civilians."[77]

These are lies, and the whole world knows it. But Hamas claiming the term "Islamic values" should cause particular concern. Hamas takes literally the prophet Muhammed's admonition to kill Jews, as stated in a handful of verses in the Quran and the Hadith (a collection of Mohammed's sayings). These verses occur later in the Quran's narrative. To many Islamic scholars, this means that they have greater authority.

> By positioning itself as a victim, Hamas forfeits its agency to the perceived object of its obstruction—Israel. Violence against Israel is a feature, not a bug, of the Hamas project.

As his life progressed, Mohammed became increasingly militant. He expressed violent sentiments toward many, including the Jews. Hamas takes these verses as clear-cut commands. To Hamas, killing Jews is a legitimate expression of "Islamic values." In fact, as we saw from the Hamas charter, anything that advances the "resistance" is seen as legitimate self-defense.

By positioning itself as a victim, Hamas forfeits its agency to the perceived object of its obstruction—Israel. Violence against Israel is a feature, not a bug, of the Hamas project. Those who commit violence in the name of the "resistance" are cherished and rewarded. Even sexual violence of the most heinous kind.

Sexual Assault as a War-Fighting Strategy

If you feel that you may be triggered by descriptions of sexual assault, you should skip this section.

The Association of Rape Crisis Centers in Israel has produced an extensive report about Hamas's strategy of employing sexual abuse in its attacks on Israeli civilians. A United Nations study group has confirmed the details of this report. It is based on thorough testimonials from eyewitnesses and those tasked with handling the bodies of Hamas's victims. It proves beyond a reasonable doubt that Hamas terrorists systematically and intentionally employed sexual abuse in the October 7 attacks.[78]

One doctor testified that the terrorists seemed "obsessed" with rape and with mutilating sexual organs. Terrorists who were killed were found with phrasebooks explaining how to say, in Hebrew, "Take your clothes off!" and "Spread your legs!"[79] The evidence shows that the sadistic Hamas terrorists gang-raped women of all ages and cut off their breasts—often with their partners, parents, or children tied up and forced to watch—before killing them. Some of the women had been raped so violently that their pelvises were broken. These were not isolated incidents. They occurred across multiple attack sites.

The academic literature on war crimes says that such strategies are used not only to destroy the dignity of female victims but also to humiliate and undermine the masculinity of men who are unable to protect them. Sexual violence is committed to sow fear and display psychological control and to inflict survivors with life-long distress and trauma. The nature of Hamas's sexual violence, as relayed by witnesses and forensic evidence, shows that Hamas intended to destroy the dignity of their victims before killing them. By sexually assaulting its victims, Hamas symbolically projected to all Israelis that they are not viewed as humans, that they will be attacked at will, and that their nation cannot protect them.

> If Hamas had done to Muslim women what it systematically and intentionally did to Jewish women, Gazans would almost certainly have slaughtered the terrorists themselves.

That Hamas shelters itself behind "Islamic values" in these actions should cause the global Islamic community to rise in outrage. If Hamas had done to Muslim women what it systematically and intentionally did to Jewish women, Gazans would almost certainly have slaughtered the terrorists themselves.

Hamas Crimes against the Palestinian People

Life in Gaza under Hamas has been a nightmare of torture, killing, fear, and suppression. According to Human Rights Watch, Hamas and its West Bank counterpart the Palestinian Authority have been "systematically mistreating and torturing Palestinians in detention, including critics and opponents." This torture "may amount to crimes against humanity, given its systematic nature over many years."[80]

Hamas's Evil Education System

Children in Gaza are indoctrinated by Hamas through curriculum in their schools, even United Nations-sponsored ones. Arnon Groiss, a former Arabic language broadcaster with a Ph.D. in Near Eastern Studies from Princeton, read and translated two hundred Palestinian textbooks used by Hamas. He found that from a young age, Gazan children are being desensitized to human life and prepared for war. Even math classes are not exempt. One math problem asks students to calculate how many Jews were killed in the first and second intifada.[81]

> From a young age, Gazan children are being desensitized to human life and prepared for war.

In literature, students studied the following poem:

> Hearing [weapons] clash is pleasant to my ear
> And the flow of blood gladdens my soul
> As well as a body thrown upon the ground
> Skirmished over by the desert predator
> By your life! This is the death of men
> And whoever asks for a noble death—this is it![82]

A history textbook describes a massacre as a "barbeque" in which terrorists hijacked a bus and murdered thirty-eight Jews, burning them alive.[83] A report by two independent researchers found that even teachers in UN-sponsored schools taught children to kill Jews. The report names and shares comments translated from UN teachers' speeches and social media posts glorifying terrorism, praising suicide bombers for their "self-sacrifice," and honoring those who have killed Jews as "heroes."[84]

A related group called Islamic Jihad runs "Revenge of the Free" summer camps for Gazan children as young as six. The camps feature military activities, including the simulated kidnapping of an Israeli soldier. The camps are used to recruit students to join militant organizations.[85] It has been said that the hand that rocks the cradle rules the world. Hamas intends to be that hand, and its education system displays exactly how it intends to rule.

Hamas's Suppression of Free Speech

As you would expect, freedom of the press under Hamas is nil. Gazan Hamza Howidy wrote in *Newsweek*, "Voicing dissent was not an option.

Hamas has a no-tolerance policy for criticism or objections to any of its policies. Even discussion is forbidden. Any journalist who objects or criticizes a policy is suspended and investigated. Demonstrations are strictly prohibited. Freedom of speech in Gaza is a fantasy."[86]

Yossi Klein Halevi, an activist who promotes peace between Israel and Palestine, wrote in his book *Letters to My Palestinian Neighbor*, "I understand that it's far easier for the victor to show nuance than the vanquished. Still, in all the years I've been following Palestinian media, I don't recall a single op-ed or editorial in any publication, regardless of its political affiliation, advocating a reassessment of the Jewish narrative. Not one article among the daily media assault denying and ridiculing and denouncing my being."[87]

Even Amnesty International, a group that sympathizes with the Palestinian people and regularly criticizes Israel, admits that there is no independent media in Palestinian territories and that dissenting journalists are brutally repressed.[88]

> Hamas is well-armed and trained by Iran and lavishly funded by gullible nations and state sponsors of terror, such as Qatar.

Given this, what do you think the chances are that Hamas is telling the truth about what is happening in Gaza? For decades, Hamas maintained its dictatorial chokehold on Gaza in full view of the international community. How was this possible? The answer is that it is well-armed and trained by Iran and lavishly funded by gullible nations and state sponsors of terror, such as Qatar. Let's look at each in turn.

Iran: How to Arm a "Resistance"

Iran is the fourth richest country in the world in terms of oil reserves and second in natural gas. Its primary customer is China, which purchases 90 percent of its fossil fuel products. Iran avoids blockades of its oil by having its ships turn off their transponders at sea and, through a complex series of transactions, brands its oil as being from other Middle Eastern countries or Malaysia.[89]

The Council on Foreign Relations says that Iran annually gives $100 million to Hamas and other Palestinian terrorist groups. Its foreign ministry spokesman Nassar Kanani praised Hamas's October 7 slaughter and recently pledged Iran's continuing support.[90] After October 7, Iranian television showed members of parliament chanting "Death to Israel" and "Palestine is victorious."[91]

> Hamas leaders have become millionaires and billionaires. Where does all this money come from?

Iranian security officials admit that Iran provided rockets to Hamas and showed its fighters how to build their own.[92] CNN reported that the Iranian Islamic Revolutionary Guard Corps "has been giving Hamas engineers weapons training for almost two decades."[93] Weapons from Iran are shipped to Somalia or Sudan and then smuggled overland through Egypt and into Gaza through tunnels.[94]

The weapons provided by Iran include Qassam rockets that have been launched by the tens of thousands toward Israel.[95] Some of these rockets can travel up to twenty-five miles, which makes much of the state of Israel vulnerable to attack. Newer rocket models feature multiple launch systems that are claimed to hold a 130-pound warhead as well as J-80 rockets that have a fifty-mile range.[96]

Hamas also has acquired Norinco automatic rifles and rocket-propelled grenades such as RPG-7s as well as Chinese Type 69 RPGs that are designed to defeat tank armor.[97] Additional weapons include Russian-made mortars, Kornet laser-guided anti-tank missiles that can melt through two feet of steel, and "Shahab" suicide drones designed by Iran.[98] A similar drone killed three American service members and wounded twenty-five more at a base in Jordan in January 2024.

Obviously, all this weaponry is expensive. Plus, fighters are paid handsome sums far beyond the average Gazan's salary. In Hamas's "pay to slay" arrangement, families of Palestinians who have been arrested and convicted of terror-related activities in Israel are given stipends amounting to two or three times the annual Gazan's wage. And somehow, in the process, Hamas leaders have become millionaires and billionaires. Where does all this money come from?

Qatar: How to Fund a "Resistance"

Hamas's most significant funder is the tiny but fabulously wealthy nation of Qatar. Qatar has the third largest natural gas reserve in the world. Its royal family is swimming in an ocean of money from this reserve, with a net worth estimated at $335 billion.[99] Qatar's Emir Tamim bin Hamad Al Thani, the head of the royal family, reportedly owns more real estate in London than the UK's royal family.[100]

The Council on Foreign Relations says that Qatar took in Hamas after Hamas lost its Syrian sponsorship because of a 2011 uprising of Palestinian refugees, which precipitated a civil war.[101] Qatar says that its goal is to help Hamas become a "reasonable governing power."[102] Other Arab nations find this explanation suspicious. The Gulf Cooperation Council suspended Qatar over its ties to terrorism. In 2017, Saudi Arabia, UAE, Bahrain, and Egypt severed relations with the nation.[103]

The Foundation for Defense of Democracies has reported that Qatar provides Hamas between $120 million and $480 million per year.[104] Much of this money makes its way directly into the hands of Hamas's top echelon of leadership, who have found sanctuary in Qatar's villas and five-star hotels even while Qatar receives billions from America for a military base in the country.[105] Hamas's top three leaders have a reported net worth of $11 billion.[106] Khaled Mashaal, Hamas's primary spokesperson, is estimated to have a net worth of $5 billion. He owns banks and real estate projects throughout the Middle East.[107]

If you were a leader of Hamas, would you be living a billionaire lifestyle of private jets and five-star hotels while your people are mired in misery and poverty? Apparently, Hamas's leadership has no problem with this. It's not just top Hamas leaders, either. The MacKenzie Institute says even Hamas's mid-level leaders have become millionaires due to a 20 to 25 percent "tax" on all goods brought into Gaza.[108] Some six hundred Hamas leaders have become millionaires through this graft.

It's rare to hear criticism of Qatar from Washington, DC. The US base in Qatar is considered of utmost strategic importance. Plus, Qatar spends generously on lobbying in DC—a reported $243 million since 2015. That's more than half-a-million dollars per member of Congress.[109] That kind of money apparently buys a lot of silence. Middle Eastern scholars at American universities have a lot of nice things to say about Qatar, perhaps because their beds have been well-feathered by Qatari money. Since 9/11, Qatar has been the largest foreign donor to American universities, with gifts totaling $4.7 billion.[110] The *Washington Free Beacon* places that figure at $5.7 billion.[111]

For decades, Hamas maintained a well-funded, well-armed, and brutal hold over Gazans. Some polls suggest that Gazans are just fine with this, although it is hard to imagine that people living in fear would want to tell the truth to strangers. But in a series of interviews carried out by *Foreign Affairs* magazine the week before the October 7 attacks, 44 percent of Gazans said that they had "no trust at all" in Hamas; and 23 percent said they had "not a lot of trust." Seventy-two percent of Gazans said there is a large or medium amount of corruption in Hamas.[112]

The destruction of Gaza resulting from Hamas's war with Israel may have moved Gazans toward greater support of Hamas. It certainly has among Palestinians in general, with three-fourths saying they support the October 7 attacks.[113] But my Arab friends assure me that when Hamas is defeated, Gazans will dance in the streets. Either way, it is clearly in the interests of the larger Palestinian cause for Hamas to be stopped, not celebrated.

Hamas has become a pariah, even in strongly Islamic nations. UAE, Bahrain, and Egypt have all outlawed it. Saudi Arabia has jailed all the Hamas leaders it has found. None of the non-terrorist Middle Eastern states have condoned the October 7 attacks. And even the famously left-leaning International Court of Justice declined to order a cease-fire on Israel's attacks in Gaza.

Yes, Hamas is an evil entity run by heartless, hypocritical leaders, whose primary aim is the destruction of Israel, not the peace and prosperity of Gazans. Yet in world opinion, it is Israel, not Hamas, that is responsible for destruction resulting from the Israel/Hamas war. Israel has the backing of the United States, an advanced military, and a strong economic base. Gazans seem helpless by comparison.

This leads to a tough question: Yes, Hamas is evil, but does that make Israel's war against it just?

PART 3

FINDING
SOLUTIONS
FROM A BIBLICAL
WORLDVIEW

CHAPTER 9

Is Israel's War against Hamas Just?

To discern whether Israel's war against Hamas is just, we need to understand whether any war at all may be just. The question is not whether war is evil. It is. The question is, how might evil be minimized when war becomes inevitable?

Jesus said, "'Blessed are the peacemakers'" (Matthew 5:9). But saying "'Peace, peace,' when there is no peace" is to heal a wound lightly (Jeremiah 6:14). Evil must be opposed; peace dies when evil reigns. Evildoers must be stopped.

> The question is not whether war is evil. It is. The question is, how might evil be minimized when war becomes inevitable?

War is a part of human life. It always has been. The historian Will Durant claimed that only 268 years in recorded human history have been completely at peace. It's upsetting when our peace is disturbed; but war, not peace, is history's norm. Yet in the battle against evil, innocents are nearly always caught in the crossfire. It is a heartrending paradox. When attacked, the wolves hide among the sheep.

The questions we face are many: Is Israel's war against Hamas just? Even if it is, is Israel committing genocide, as Hamas claims? Is Israel fulfilling its obligations to protect civilians during war? Is Hamas doing the same? Are civilian casualties excessive, and does this constitute a moral demand for Israel to cease its attacks?

In the Israel/Hamas war, we think we know what is happening because we've seen the pictures. As everyone knows, a picture is worth a thousand words. But what if those words form a lie? Hamas controls all information coming out of Gaza. It adroitly manages its information flow for propaganda purposes. Yet many find themselves conflicted by the alternating display of Hamas brutality against Israel and the distress of those harmed when Israel strikes back. Hamas and its public relations operatives paint a dialectical picture of victory and victimhood, fearlessness and futility, righteousness and rage. They portray Hamas as virtuous, even as its bold brushstrokes are thickened with blood.

> Learning how our forebears were faithfully present in their moment shows us how to be faithfully present in our own.

To a postmodern mindset, if a story is being told the way it ought to be told and if it rings true, then it must be true. There is no overall point to history; there is only the present, and it is ours to shape as we please. Truth is what we say it is.

The Difference a Biblical Worldview of Conflict Makes

A biblical worldview locates truth outside of ourselves. We humans don't write the story we are in. Our goal should not be to force meaning into the present moment but to be faithfully present in whatever moments we are given. Faithful presence compels us to study history. Learning how our forebears were faithfully present in their moment shows us how to be faithfully present in our own. A biblical worldview is revelatory, not utopian. To paraphrase C. S. Lewis, the light we see is also the light by which we see everything else.

So when the question arises of what God requires of us in times of war, our answer is not to justify every action by whether it moves us closer to a desired utopian state. Instead, it is to discern what justice and faithfulness look like right now, trusting God for the outcome.

Four ways of being faithfully present in times of war have developed over the centuries. *Pacifism* says that war is never just and that no matter the larger issues at stake, believers must not be involved in any way. *Non-resistance* says that war may sometimes be just, but it is wrong for believers to be involved as combatants. *Just War Theory* says that believers may participate in war if it is a just response to an attack, according to specific criteria. *Preventive war* says that justice sometimes requires that believers act preemptively to eliminate evil forces before they can do damage.

In history, pacifism and nonresistance are admirable stances held only by small communities of believers. Biblical scholars, such as Augustine of Hippo and Thomas Aquinas, took a more prudential approach. War is evil, they wrote; yet it is also sometimes the only way to limit the spread of evil. Therefore, we are best served not by avoiding it but by carrying it out as justly as possible.

> The greatest evil of war is not that people die. We all die. The greatest evil is that greed, lust, and generational hatred might be allowed to rain down misery on the innocent, preventing them from living integral lives as God intended.

"Even wars have rules," says the International Red Cross. This means "you do not attack civilians. You limit as much as you can the impact of your warfare on women and children, as well as on other civilians. You treat detainees humanely. You do not torture people."[114]

How Can War, Being Evil, Ever Be Conducted Justly?

Augustine and Aquinas did not believe that the greatest evil of war was that people die. We all die. The greatest evil was that greed, lust, and generational hatred might be allowed to rain down misery on the innocent, preventing them from living integral lives as God intended. A shameful peace based on nonaction is not to be preferred to a just peace based on action.

Starting with a view of humans as God's image-bearers, Augustine and Aquinas developed several principles of what constitutes a just war.[115] These principles come down to three things, according to just-war expert Eric Patterson:

1. War is declared by a legitimate government,

2. Acting on a just cause,

3. With right intention.[116]

How does Israel's actions against Hamas stack up against these three principles? Israel is a legitimate government. It did not act militarily against Hamas without being attacked. Its declared intent was to secure the release of its hostages and to end Hamas's rule, not to destroy the Gazan population. This aim seems justified based on the history of the situation and the nature of Hamas itself.

Rachel Goldberg, whose son was taken captive by Hamas on October 7: "If you only care when one side's babies die, your moral compass is broken."

Still, the goal of Just War Theory is not to justify war but to secure justice in the context of war. The line between injustice and justice is appallingly easy to cross. Though most of the world acknowledges that justice will never be secure until Hamas is eliminated, it is easy to turn our hearts away from the innocent who find themselves in the crossfire because of their proximity to the evildoers. We cannot let the justness of war drain us of compassion. As Rachel Goldberg, whose son was taken captive by Hamas on October 7, puts it, "If you only care when one side's babies die, your moral compass is broken."[117]

War and the Value of Every Life

How does Just War Theory square with Matthew 5:39, where Jesus says that if someone slaps you on the cheek, you should "'turn to him the other also'"? The philosopher Arthur Holmes (1924-2011) maintained that the context of that verse refers to individuals, not to governments or churches. "It means that as an individual I do not take the law into my own hands," he says. [118] Justice matters. National defense and law enforcement are permitted. Personal vengeance is not.

All humans are made to bear God's image. Human life is of inestimable value. A famous Mishnah in the tractate of Sanhedrin says, "One life is like a universe. Save a life and you save a universe; destroy a life and you destroy a universe."[119]

As of this writing, more than thirty thousand Gazans have been reported by Hamas's Gaza Health Ministry as having been killed in the war between Hamas and Israel. The world community takes this figure at face value, despite Hamas's obvious willingness to employ treachery if Israel's interests will be harmed thereby. Abraham Wyner, a University of Pennsylvania statistician, has analyzed the health ministry's figures and concluded, based on the way the deaths were reported, that they are "statistically impossible."[120]

A further complication is that the Hamas-controlled Gaza Health Ministry refuses to distinguish between combatant and noncombatant deaths. It maintains that *all* Gazans who die are "victims of Israel's aggression."[121] There are no combatants, only martyrs. Those who died with weapons in their hands were innocent victims engaging in justifiable self-defense, as far as Hamas is concerned.

> The Gaza Health Ministry will not distinguish between combatant and noncombatant deaths because it believes that there *are* no combatants, only innocent martyrs engaged in legitimate self-defense.

Israel defines a combatant as someone who engages in fighting during a war. It places the figure of Hamas combatants killed at well over twelve thousand. It seems plausible that Israel would be more likely to know, given the systematic way it has prosecuted the war and the rules of engagement to which it binds itself. I asked one Israeli soldier how he knows the difference between terrorists and civilians. "The terrorists are the ones that shoot at us," was his straightforward reply.

Still, many of the dead are known to have been women and children, most likely noncombatants by the standard definition. Many of these were killed by Israeli weapons of war targeted at combatants. Some entire neighborhoods have been turned to rubble. It is reasonable to ask whether the destruction of cities and the deaths of tens of thousands constitutes just retribution for the twelve hundred Israelis killed in the October 7 attack or whether some more nefarious purpose is being served.

For many, the number of civilian casualties in Gaza clearly seems to be disproportionate to the threat. If more than thirty thousand Palestinians have been killed in response to fewer than two thousand Israelis deaths, the thinking goes, then rightful vindication has become wrongful vengeance.

Do the Number of Deaths Make a War Unjust?

Knowing that war is inevitable in a fallen world, three criteria have been developed for determining whether a nation's actions *in* war are just.

Military necessity. Is the military using all lawful means to achieve tactical victory? This is a question of stewardship, the biblical idea of counting the cost. Are weapons deployed as accurately as possible? Are troops being appropriately protected?

A commander focused on military necessity doesn't see the world the way a naïve peace activist does. He doesn't say, "The enemy is hiding in tunnels, so we need to send our soldiers in one at a time and take the same risks they are." This would be immoral if another means exists that lowers the risk to his troops, such as a targeted air strike.

> Proportionality is not based on the number of casualties but on the nature of the threat. Hamas's threat to Israel has been going on for decades, and it continues even now.

Proportionality. Proportionality is not based on the number of casualties but on the nature of the threat. Hamas's threat to Israel has been going on for decades, and it continues even now. Hamas won't release the hostages and continues shooting rockets at and conducting terrorist acts in Israel. It deploys a well-developed propaganda mechanism that is actively trying to inflame world opinion against Israel. It is backed by Iran, a nation whose escalating military aggression and sponsorship of the region's most destabilizing forces represent Israel's greatest existential threat.

Ghazi Hamad, a Hamas political leader, has promised that Hamas will attack Israel "again and again" until it is destroyed.[122] Every time Hamas has the opportunity to make good on this promise, it has done so. Israel has concluded—and the world has grudgingly agreed—that neither Israel nor the Palestinian people will ever be safe as long as Hamas remains powerful.

In addition, we must consider the deterrent effect of Israel's actions against Gaza. To Israel's north, Hezbollah terrorists who control Lebanon make daily threats and back them up with rocket strikes. What keeps Hezbollah's one hundred thousand fighters from storming into Israel? Armies won't attack if they stand to lose more than they stand to gain. Hezbollah knows that Israel will defend itself aggressively if attacked. Iran, which controls Hezbollah, may not care whether Lebanon is destroyed; but it does care that its own infrastructure is not attacked by a nuclear-capable Israel.

> Every time Hamas has had the opportunity to make good on its promise to destroy Israel, it has done so.

By historical comparison, Israel's offensive in Gaza is blistering yet restrained. Typically, in an urban warfare situation such as that in Gaza, civilians account for 90 percent of casualties.[123] Using the Gaza Health Ministry numbers and Israel's reporting about how many of the dead were combatants, one or two civilians have died for every combatant killed. This is far, far lower than the average and approximately the same civilian death rate as World War II and Vietnam, in a much more complex situation.

Distinction. Is the military taking active measures to protect noncombatants? Part of the reason civilian casualties have been much lower than historical norms is that the IDF operates by rules of engagement designed to limit civilian casualties. It uses precision weapons to focus on specific targets. It alerts residents to evacuate areas that will be targeted. As of this writing, since October 7, the IDF has made seventy-nine thousand phone calls, sent 13.7 million texts, dropped 7.2 million pamphlets, made fifteen million recorded phone calls, and evacuated 1.2 million Gazans to safe zones.[124] John Spencer, a leading expert on urban warfare, says that "Israel has implemented more precautions to prevent civilian harm than any military in history—above and beyond what international law requires and more than the United States did in its wars in Iraq and Afghanistan."[125]

America's leaders may have strong disagreements with Israel's current government, but they continue to provide military assistance because they know that the IDF is prosecuting the war as justly as possible. The White House spokesperson on foreign policy and national security John Kirby said that it's "obvious to us" that Israel is "trying to minimize" civilian casualties and said that unlike Russia's attack against Ukraine and Hamas's attack of October 7, it is not a war aim of Israel to attack civilians.[126]

Israel's response fits within the norms of what would be expected in a similar situation at another time in another part of the world. Some people will still oppose Israel's actions, but it isn't because Israel is prosecuting the war differently than we would expect another nation to be in a similar situation. It must be for some other reason.

Is Hamas Conducting a Just War?

Has Hamas acted in a similarly just fashion? The answer is clearly no. Hamas does not distinguish between combatants and noncombatants in Gaza, though it does consider all Israelis to be combatants. Nor does Hamas act in a way that is proportional to the threat. Murdering and raping innocents and desecrating their bodies violates the very essence of just war. If you meet anyone who thinks these actions are justified, you should probably question the basis upon which they make *any* claims about the war. Their moral compass is clearly broken.

Human Shields

Further, Hamas has displayed no regard for noncombatants caught in the war zone. Indeed, Hamas hides behind them as human shields, something that anti-Israel activists have cynically taken to calling "asymmetrical warfare," to deflect from what it manifestly is: hiding behind civilians. In a Department of Defense publication, Air Force Brigadier General Pat Ryder said, "We know that Hamas is integrating its operations, whether it's command and control, operational centers, combat forces, putting rockets in Gaza, to include this complex and sprawling tunnel network underneath infrastructure throughout Gaza, in effect... using civilians as human shields."[127]

This is not a new situation. *NGO Monitor* says that for years, "Hamas has systematically exploited the civilian population of Gaza as 'human shields,' expecting that their presence will either deter Israeli attacks or result in large numbers of civilian casualties providing a PR victory and generating international pressure, condemnations, and sanctions against Israel."[128]

An intelligence officer our group spoke with in Israel analyzed Arab media posts and found evidence that Hamas kills those who refuse to be human shields. This is not an accusation; it is something Hamas fighters have bragged about on social media. A Palestinian news agency reported that Hamas executed dozens of Palestinians suspected of collaborating with Israel.[129] The Jewish Telegraphic Agency, a wire service for Jewish news, has persistently reported on this. The mainstream media typically doesn't see it as an important part of the story.

Remember, Hamas—based on its charter—believes that anything it does to advance the "resistance" constitutes legitimate self-defense. This includes shielding its forces with its own citizens to discourage Israeli attacks. The human shield strategy is common not only with Hamas but also with other terrorist groups, such as ISIS and the Taliban. The Taliban was known to hide its combatants in civilians' homes and in hospitals and to store its weapons in mosques. In the battle of Mosul, ISIS fighters forced one hundred thousand civilians together to shield themselves from government forces.[130]

Hamas has also killed many civilians with rockets intended for Israel that instead landed in civilian areas. The Foundation for Defense of Democracies reported on a study of one IDF operation in Gaza in which fifteen of the twenty-six Palestinian civilians killed were killed by Palestinian rockets that landed in its own territory and only eleven by the IDF.[131] The analysis showed that 18 percent of the rockets fired by Palestinians in that conflict hit Palestinian areas rather than their intended targets in Israel.[132]

> Hamas believes that anything it does to advance the "resistance" constitutes legitimate self-defense. This includes shielding its forces with its own citizens to discourage Israeli attacks.

Israel says that it has little choice but to continue its attacks. If Hamas retains the ability to reconstitute itself, it has publicly promised that its fighters will repeat the October 7 attacks as many times as they can and "from wherever they can."[133] Khaled Mashaal, the billionaire "external leader" of Hamas who is a godlike figure to Hamas's leadership because he once survived an assassination attempt and imprisonment, said in a publicly available interview that any plans for peace for Israel would be to "establish common ground" with other Palestinian groups so they can unite together for Israel's abolition. He bragged that Hamas's control of Gaza has provided it "political and administrative cover" to manufacture weapons, dig tunnels, and train its members without being disturbed by Israel or by the Palestinian Authority.[134]

> Hamas has publicly displayed a willingness to sacrifice as many Gazans as it thinks is necessary to annihilate Israel.

Hamas has also publicly displayed a willingness to sacrifice Gazans if it serves the larger aim of annihilating Israel. Mashaal publicly described the October 7 attack as a clever form of self-defense and resistance. He told the interviewer, "We know very well the consequences of our operation on October 7." He pointed to the millions who died in in Russia, Vietnam, Afghanistan, and Algeria in pursuit of revolutionary aims and crowed, "Dear sister, the Palestinian nation is just like any other nation. No nation is liberated without sacrifices."[135]

Clearly, Hamas cares little about Gazans or the Palestinian people in general, except that they give it the power to achieve its aim of destroying Israel. This is exactly what you would expect from an apocalyptic rape-and-death cult.

We live in a fallen world. And yet, from a biblical worldview, we must still seek justice. The reality of crime doesn't mean that we can't have effective policing. The reality of corruption doesn't mean that we can't have accountability. In the same way, the reality of war doesn't mean that justice is impossible.

Yet many still insist that the way Israel prosecutes war is not just to kill enemy combatants but to eliminate the Palestinian people. The war is just cover for genocide, they say. Does this claim have merit? Let's examine it and see.

CHAPTER 10

Charges of **Genocide**

In the last chapter, we talked about what makes a war just and the principles that must guide the use of force. Again, Just War Theory is not designed to justify war but to ensure that the war is being carried out by a legitimate authority, with a just cause, and in view of protecting noncombatants as much as possible. You probably won't see any news articles analyzing whether Israel's war against Hamas meets the principles of just war. But you almost certainly will hear of Israel's actions being described as genocide.

Charges of Genocide Began before Israel's Military Response

I'll share the internationally accepted definition of genocide in a moment; but for now, we can say that genocide occurs when a government intentionally targets a people group for extinction. The charges of genocide against Israel began immediately after the October 7 Hamas attack and before Israel launched a military response beyond killing the attacking terrorists and striking known rocket launch sites and terrorist hideouts. As we've already seen, Students for Justice in Palestine released a statement accusing Israel of genocide before Israel had responded militarily.

On October 8, a group called Churches for Middle East Peace (CMEP)—whose members include the Evangelical Lutheran Church, the Reformed Church in America, the American Baptists, the Episcopal Church, the United Methodist Church, and the Presbyterian Church (USA)—called for an immediate cease-fire and condemned Israel for "ethnic cleansing."[136] CMEP's call for an immediate cease-fire may make its members feel righteous about their desire for peace, but it ignores how difficult situations are resolved in the real world. Good intentions are not enough to make good policy.

At the same time, statements calling for Israel to stop attacking Hamas expose a worldview bias. Since Israel hadn't taken any significant action in its war against Hamas when SJP's and CMEP's messages were released, the charges of genocide and ethnic cleansing must have been based on...what? We have enough information from these groups and others like them to give a provisional answer: they *assume* either that Israel has no right to exist or that its actions against enemies are unjust. If Israel is not legitimate, then it cannot meet the very first criteria for conducting a just war. Any actions it takes to defeat its enemies are, by definition, war crimes.

South Africa's Genocide Suit against Israel

War crimes are exactly what Israel is being accused of. These accusations came to a head when the Republic of South Africa filed suit against Israel in the International Court of Justice (ICJ) claiming that by attacking

Hamas in urban areas of Gaza, Israel was committing genocide. In its ruling, the ICJ warned Israel to take measures to limit civilian casualties but stopped short of accusing Israel of genocide, or ordering a cease-fire.

Is Israel genuinely guilty of genocide or was South Africa's suit some kind of a ploy? The question sounds cynical, but the fuzzy math of international relations demands that we ask tough questions. What was behind South Africa's filing of this suit? Why South Africa, of all nations? According to a Harvard study, South Africa is rapidly becoming a failed state under the leadership of the African National Congress (ANC).[137] Its four largest cities have joined the list of the world's murder capitals; public services have collapsed; and economic and gender inequality have greatly increased.[138]

South Africa was supposed to be a story of rising above racial hatred to become a force for good. Nelson Mandela's journey from prison to the presidency inspired the world. Mandela fought against apartheid, or separatism, the doctrine that tension between races would best be solved by racial separation. Racialism is, sadly, practiced by nearly every society. But it seemed particularly egregious in South Africa because it was practiced by white people against black and colored (the South African term for people who aren't white or black) people.

In the late '90s, before the rise of Hamas, Mandela weighed in on the Israel/Palestine divide: "Our freedom is incomplete without the freedom of the Palestinians."[139] At the same time, though, Mandela insisted that Israel has a right to exist, a position that both the PLO and Hamas explicitly reject. Mandela's successors have each made South Africa worse. And now, by allying with the very terrorist group that oppresses the Palestinian people, the African National Congress has unraveled his legacy.

South Africa's primary international partners are Iran, Russia, and China—all backers of Hamas. The ANC has a close and public relationship with Hamas, sealed through two memoranda of understanding in 2015 and 2018. In an op-ed in Israel's *Haaretz* newspaper, which is anything but a conservative publication, South African Jew Mary Kluk derided the "pornographic, sycophantic romance between [South Africa's] government ministers and Hamas."[140]

Plus, South Africa's president, Cyril Ramaphosa, has repeatedly defied and condemned the very court system South Africa used to file its suit. In 2015, Ramaphosa hosted as an honored guest the convicted war criminal Omar al-Bashir, Sudan's deposed president. He was obligated by South Africa's membership in the International Criminal Court (the counterpart of the International Court of Justice) to arrest al-Bashir but refused. Even as it pressed its case at the ICJ in January 2024, Ramaphosa played host to the notorious Sudanese war criminal Muhammad Hamdan Dagalo.[141]

To be sure, the international courts are notoriously unreliable, aligned with anti-western powers, and without any enforcement authority. Dozens of countries are not members—including the United States. As late as August 2023, Ramaphosa insisted that South Africa should dissolve its relationship with the international courts as well. So it was surprising when South Africa did an about-face in not only supporting the international courts but also in filing a suit against Israel in those very venues. Several commentators and human rights organizations found the following timeline of South Africa's filing suspicious:

- Before the October 7 Hamas attack took place, the ANC was bankrupt with a court judgment of $5.4 million against it. With its social services suspended and salaries going unpaid, it looked as if the ANC would have to liquidate.
- On December 22, 2023, the ANC's debt was mysteriously paid and a settlement announced.[142]
- One week later, on December 29, South Africa filed the case against Israel in the International Court of Justice (ICJ).[143]
- A week and a half after that, on January 10, 2024, Iran publicly praised South Africa's "responsible, courageous, and honorable move" in filing the case.[144]

Within nineteen days the ANC went from bankruptcy to being viewed as the world's guardian of morality. ANC leaders insist it's a coincidence. But it is widely believed among South Africans that Iran paid off the ANC's debt in exchange for bringing up the charge of genocide in the ICJ. The ANC leaders' warm relationship with Iran makes this plausible. While most of the world condemns Iran for its oppressive theocracy and well-documented human rights abuses, South African foreign minister Naledi Pandor defended it, stating that "I don't know whether they are an authoritarian regime."[145]

This taint of corruption may explain why even the notably leftist ICJ refused to accuse Israel of genocide, did not call for a cease-fire in Israel's campaign against Hamas, and rejected South Africa's later request to put more pressure on Israel to stop fighting. Only time will tell whether the ANC's three-week reversal of fortunes is on the up and up. I've met people who are imaginative enough to believe that it is. But among South Africa's observers, there are many who think it reeks of hypocrisy and exemplifies the lengths to which triumphalist anti-Israel forces will go to make their point. International politics can be a very strange game.

But political machinations aside, the problem about genocide remains. Yes, Hamas is a corrupt power that has managed to ally itself with every unscrupulous plutocrat who could scrape up a few bucks or a few weapons. Yet Gazan noncombatants continue to die. Isn't that genocide? To understand how to approach this question, we need to look at what genocide is, based on international norms agreed to by both Israel and the Palestinians.

What Is Genocide?

Genocide became an international concern in the aftermath of the Second World War, when it became clear that both Germany and Russia had acted to intentionally kill as many Jews as possible, as well as citizens of nations such as Poland. In response, the United Nations held the Convention on the Prevention and Punishment of the Crime of Genocide. The resulting agreement took force in 1951. It defined genocide in the following way:

> In the present Convention, genocide means any of the following acts committed with intent to destroy, in whole or in part, a national, ethnical, racial or religious group, as such: (a) Killing members of the group; (b) Causing serious bodily or mental harm to members of the group; (c) Deliberately inflicting on the group conditions of life calculated to bring about its physical destruction in whole or in part; (d) Imposing measures intended to prevent births within the group; (e) Forcibly transferring children of the group to another group.[146]

Deliberate intent is the key. For genocide to occur, according to the deliberations of the International Court of Justice, "the intent must be to destroy at least a substantial part of the particular group."[147] To prove intent, the accuser must show something beyond cultural destruction, dispersion of people, or attacks on individuals from the group. It must be shown that there was an organized plan or policy designed to deliberately target the group itself.[148]

In its defense at the ICJ, Israel said that not only did it not intentionally target Palestinian civilians in Gaza but that hostilities were decreasing as Israel achieved its stated war goals. It said that in addition to its strict rules of engagement, it had actively provided humanitarian assistance in Gaza through opening a dozen bakeries that produced two million loaves of bread a day, delivering its own water to Gaza through two pipelines as well as taking other measures to ensure water delivery, and facilitating six field hospitals and two floating hospitals with more being constructed. Israel says that it is evacuating the ill and wounded through the Rafah border crossing and has distributed tents, winter equipment, fuel, and cooking gas.[149]

> For genocide to occur, according to the deliberations of the International Court of Justice, "the intent must be to destroy at least a substantial part of the particular group."

To the charge that Israel was committing genocide by displacing Gazans from their homes, Israel points out that Rule 129 from the Genocide Convention specifies that the civilian population may not be forcibly transferred "unless the security of the civilians involved or imperative military reasons so demand."[150] Israel says that this demand has been met and that it has complied with this aspect of the convention.

During its war with Hamas, Israel has been accused of starving Gazans as a tool of genocide. The charge is now known to be false. Columbia University business school professors Awi Fedengruen and Ran Kivetz analyzed the aid situation and reported that enough food was delivered to Gaza between October 2023 and April 2024—290,000 tons—to meet 50 percent of Gaza's food needs, even as three-fourths of Gaza's agricultural production ability remains intact. If people aren't getting enough food, Hamas theft is the most likely culprit.[151]

Hypocrisy in Claims of Genocide

At the time of my January 2024 trip to Israel, the ICJ case between South Africa and Israel had not been decided. Yet the Israelis I spoke to were skeptical that they could get a fair hearing, given the international prejudice repeatedly displayed against Israel in international venues. An opinion piece in the *Jerusalem Post* noted that while groups like Amnesty International call out Ukraine for operating in urban areas and endangering civilians, the group seemed uninterested in addressing that exact tactic by Hamas or Islamic jihad.[152]

One official gloomily summarized the underlying message the international community seems to be sending: "When the Jew is dead, we love him; when he is strong, we hate him."

Israelis also point out that if the displacement of a people group counts as genocide, then Hamas's stated aim of killing Jews unquestionably meets the definition. Also, they point to the Islamic genocide against Jews that has continued unabated since 1948. In 1948, Egypt was home to seventy-five thousand Jews. Now fewer than one hundred are there. There are no Jews left in Libya and Algeria, both of which had populations of tens of thousands in 1948. At that time, there were 850,000 Jews in the Middle East and North Africa, outside of Israel. Fewer than ten thousand remain.[153] Most of these Jews presumably emigrated to Israel. But according to the World Organization of Jews from Arab Countries, they had to leave behind land and assets worth more than $300 billion, wealth that was confiscated by the various governments from which they fled.[154] These same Arab countries, not coincidentally, have also ensured that Palestinians remain stateless. None, except Israel, are offering any kind of citizenship to Palestinians.[155]

> One official gloomily summarized the underlying message the international community seems to be sending: "When the Jew is dead, we love him; when he is strong, we hate him."

If the facts are as clear as what we've seen so far in this book, you might be wondering why so many people are misled. Even if you disagree with much of what I've said, you probably share my concern about the impact of propaganda on today's society. Let's turn to that topic now.

CHAPTER II

The **Propaganda** War

It's called "the fog of war." Confusion and uncertainty reign in the mind, even as weaponry rains down death on the body. The facts surrounding Israel's war against Hamas—and about the Israel/Palestine conflict in general—are especially foggy. Terms like "white settler colonialism," "genocide," "ethnic cleansing," and "apartheid" charge the issue emotionally, making it difficult to discern fact from fiction.

Are these accusations just hyperbole born of passionate emotions, or is there something more going on? In 1999, the French journalist Baudouin Loos interviewed Israeli-born professor Ilan Pappé, an avowed Marxist. It is Pappé's controversial work that planted the seed that Israel is best understood as an illegitimate colonialist settler state bent on ethnic cleansing.

Unlike many anti-Israel activists, Pappé is unusually forthright about his lack of objectivity: "There is no historian in the world who is objective. I am not as interested in what happened as in how people see what happened."[156] When Loos asked for the facts behind his claims, Pappé' replied, "The struggle is about ideology, not about facts... Who knows what the facts are? We try to convince as many people as we can that our interpretation of the facts is the correct one, and we do it because of ideological reasons, not because we are truth-seekers."[157]

> A "post-truth" perspective destroys the tools with which the international community attempts to carve out clarity amidst competing claims of truth.

Of course, just because one historian is careless about facts doesn't mean all anti-Israel activists are propagandists, rather than truth-seekers. But it does highlight a core concern with how a "post-truth" perspective destroys the tools with which the international community attempts to carve out clarity amidst competing claims of truth. It's frustrating to present the facts as objectively as possible only to have people say, "I guess it's a matter of perspective" or "Who really knows what's true?" People say things like, "One man's terrorist is another man's freedom fighter." This kind of sloppy analysis is both lazy and dangerous. Real lives are at stake.

If all truth is relative to the situation, then who's to say whether there is any such thing as pure persuasion? Maybe all persuasive messages are mere propaganda. If so, clarity is impossible. All we have are competing viewpoints. But is it really the case that no valid distinctions can be made?

Is All Persuasion Just Propaganda?

A famous proverb says, "When words are many, transgression is not lacking" (Proverbs 10:19). The sheer volume of words devoted to the Israel/Hamas war naturally gives rise to propaganda, as opposed to ethical persuasion. Is it possible to know the difference? Let's define each term. Persuasion is using ethical arguments to move people closer to the truth. Propaganda is using any argument (ethical or unethical) to move people closer to *your viewpoint*. Persuasion is about insight. Propaganda is about power.

If someone tells you that the truth is not knowable by you, there's a better than even chance that everything they say after that is propaganda. Telling you that *you* cannot know the truth (but they *can*) is the basis of every lie.

Persuasion experts Anthony Pratkanis and Elliot Aronson define propaganda as follows:

- Mass "suggestion" or "influence" through the manipulation of symbols and the psychology of the individual,
- The dexterous use of images, slogans, and symbols that play on our prejudices and emotions,
- The communication of a point of view with the ultimate goal of having the recipient of the appeal come to "voluntarily" accept this position as if it were his or her own.[158]

Hamas's PR campaign surrounding its October 7 military campaign is a master class in propaganda. As we've already seen, the PR and the military campaigns were executed nearly simultaneously. Students for Justice in Palestine was so prepared for the campaign that it hosted a nationwide "Day of Resistance" just five days after Hamas's brutal attack. Coordinators were alerted *on the day of the attack* to join for a planning call.

The evidence that propaganda was at play became obvious when SJP's PR messaging memo was leaked.[159] It is a hodgepodge of Hamas talking points and Marxist mumbo jumbo, describing the

> Persuasion is about insight. Propaganda is about power.

October 7 attack as a "prison break" and claiming that the Israeli "settlers" were military assets, not civilians. It also claimed that Israel was fragile and on the point of breaking and that all means of resistance, including armed struggle, is "legitimate" and "necessary." All of this is lifted concept for concept and, in many cases, word for word from Hamas's charter. Even SJP's chant "glory to our resistance" is a well-known Hamas war cry.

SJP provided coordinators a "toolkit," available almost immediately after the October 7 attack, that included a Palestinian flag and a poster of a terrorist swooping down on an unsuspecting crowd in a paraglider, which is one of the ways the October 7 terrorists penetrated the Israel border that day.[160] The toolkit stated, "We as Palestinian students in exile are PART of this movement…not in solidarity with this movement."[161] If the participating students knew they were supporting Hamas, then they are guilty of aiding terrorism. If they did not know, then they are guilty of breathtaking ignorance of the sort that enables evil to thrive.

Who Is Behind the Pro-Hamas Propaganda?

Propaganda costs money. Follow the money and you can get a pretty good sense of the ideologies at play. In the wake of the October 7 attacks, it came to light that billionaire financier George Soros—an anti-Israel Jew—had given groups supporting the Hamas rallies $15 million.[162] This is an open secret if you're willing to spend five minutes looking at the website for Soros-funded groups like the Open Society Foundations, where a list of grantees and the grant amounts are dutifully listed.

> Propaganda costs money. Follow the money and you can get a pretty good sense of the ideologies at play.

One of the funded groups is the Foundation for Middle East Peace (FMEP), which also receives money from the Rockefeller Brothers Fund.[163] FMEP has its hands in all sorts of ventures, including grants to Churches for Middle East Peace (CMEP), the organization we talked about in the chapter on genocide.[164]

You don't have to be a conspiracy theorist to see that there are monied interests involved whose motives are suspicious. In this case, one thing, and one thing only, ties these groups together: they present themselves as pro-Palestinian, but their real agenda is anti-Israel. Their anti-Israel actions include harassing Jews, fomenting criticism of Israel, boycotting companies that do business with Israel, pressuring organizations and investment firms to withdraw their investments from Israel, and promoting the end of free trade agreements with Israel. Most of these groups are small—or, at least, they were until they received huge cash infusions from foundations controlled by Soros.

Here's an example of how the propaganda program works. On the very day of the October 7 attacks, CMEP issued a press release referring to the Jewish communities of southern Israel as "settlers," implying that Israel does not have a right to the land. It accused Israel of dangerous "nationalization" and "radicalization" and called for the United States to stop military aid. It benignly describes Hamas's bloody atrocities as an "escalation of fighting between Israel and Hamas." Rather than condemn the Hamas attacks, CMEP issued a general condemnation against "all acts of violence against civilians." This is a curious phrasing. Why not just say "Israelis" or "Jews"? Does CMEP think, as Hamas does, that Israeli "settlers" count as military personnel, not civilians? The following day, CMEP expressed concern that "Israel's response is disproportionate," while accusing it of "ethnic cleansing."[165] At the time of the press release, Israel hadn't even responded to Hamas, except to kill terrorist infiltrators and strike known rocket launch sites and terrorist hideouts.

Hamas's propaganda efforts and those of its minions in the United States are nothing new. The Program on Extremism at George Washington University has been tracking them for years and providing detailed and documented information that is publicly available.[166] Hamas's PR campaigns after October 7 clearly fit the definition of propaganda. They manipulate symbols and slogans to play on prejudices and emotions, the goal of which is to leverage people's natural sympathy for beleaguered Palestinians into support for a brutal terrorist regime.

If Hamas's propaganda message and techniques are well-known— and they are—how on earth do people fall for them? Are they stupid? Are they evil? Is there something more at play?

How Propaganda Leads to Indoctrination and Mind Control

In my decades of working with young adults who are often susceptible to false messages, I believe there is a clearer—and more charitable—explanation than to call people stupid or evil. It is this: often people become indoctrinated in the same way that people in cults are misled. It's mind control.

It's easy to imagine how an apocalyptic rape-and-death cult such as Hamas could control the minds of people in a place like Gaza. Isolated from the world and indoctrinated for decades, it would be surprising if Gazans *didn't* fall for Hamas's lies. Ideology festers in isolation. But there is a kind of self-imposed isolation that people put on themselves when they feel that they don't fit in or when they yearn for escape from their present circumstances. Using the internet, such people can quickly

Escape from mind control is difficult. It's hard to escape from a prison in which you don't realize you're imprisoned.

find affirming messages from those who "explain" their circumstances ("This! This! This!") and make them feel included ("Oh, that's *so me*!"). They might be shocked at first by the radical nature of these messages; but they quickly desensitize and begin believing that their parents, friends, and church have been lying to them or holding them back. Escape from this kind of mind control is difficult. It's hard to escape from a prison in which you don't realize you're imprisoned.

According to Steven Hassan, a therapist who helps people escape from mind control cults, mind control is "any *system* of influence that disrupts an individual's authentic identity and replaces it with a false new one."[167] Mind control emphasizes dependence and reacts strongly to independent thought. It demands conformity and makes individuality seem selfish or even evil. Hassan claims that cults work because they control behavior, information, thoughts, and emotions (B.I.T.E.):[168]

- **Behavior control** means the regulation of a person's physical reality. Cults make demands on people that leave them little time or space to act as authentic selves.

- **Information control** means positioning people to *only* pay attention to the group's messages and to dismiss contrary messaging as—ironically—propaganda.

- **Thought control** means giving people a new way of thinking and talking about reality itself using "loaded language" to condense, label, and reduce all thoughts to cliches. This is what literary critic Lionel Trilling called the "language of nonthought."

- **Emotional control** is narrowing the range of a person's feelings so that they become desensitized to anything that does not affirm the group's messaging.

Cults subtly change members' sense of space and time so that they feel as if they are living in a parallel reality in which others just don't "get it." They tell themselves that everyone outside their group is unenlightened. This sense of superiority is easily weaponized, as it was in 1994 when the leaders of Rwanda's Hutu tribe coaxed their followers to think of rival Tutsis as "cockroaches." Neighbors remorselessly slaughtered neighbors. Church members hacked to death those they had worshiped with the week before.

In the aftermath of the destruction wrought by violent Nazi, imperialist, and communist ideologies in the 1950s, psychologists sought to understand how these ideologies had captured so many minds. Robert J. Lifton, a psychiatrist and expert on the psychology of political violence, wrote that radical groups thrive through "ideological totalism," which is the taking over of a person's mind or physical circumstances so thoroughly that they cannot imagine any subject or any situation in which their new ideology does not explain *everything*.

Ideological totalism can be so complete that the more evidence there is against the dogma, the more its firmest adherents believe it. In *When Prophecy Fails*, psychologist Leon Festinger describes his research into a Wisconsin cult leader who convinced her followers that a flying saucer would arrive at a particular date and time to rescue them from a coming apocalypse. They quit their jobs, sold their possessions, and gathered in great excitement. The flying saucer didn't show up. A few of the marginal followers became discouraged and quit the group. But the firmest adherents—those who had sacrificed the most for their beliefs—became even more committed. Comforted by the hive mind that bound them together, they readily accepted the cult leader's explanation that their willingness to sacrifice had convinced the aliens to not destroy earth after all.

How is it that the failure of the cult leader's prophecies reinforced the beliefs of the most committed members? The key was information control. Those members believed that only their cult leader could

106 | SHOULD CHRISTIANS SUPPORT ISRAEL?

communicate with the aliens. The absence of contrary evidence was interpreted as proof of her veracity.

Hamas propaganda functions in a similar way. If you believe that everything in the world needs to be seen through an oppressor/oppressed narrative and accept that Hamas is a victim of oppression, every piece of evidence you examine will almost automatically reinforce these assumptions. For its true believers, whether Islamists or Marxists, Hamas doesn't need to prove its claims. It needs only to manage the flow of information enough to ensure that it points to its own righteous suffering rather than its brutality or its betrayal of the Gazans it was supposed to lead. Every picture of destroyed buildings, every story of human suffering, then, speaks for itself. It's a gift that keeps on giving. Perhaps this is why, even though support for Hamas among Palestinians has dropped goes up and down in response to news reports, seven in ten of them believe Hamas's decision to attack Israel was the right one.[169]

Propaganda from Inside the Gates

So how does Hamas manage the information flow in a way that reinforces its narrative? It is easier than you think. We Americans think we know what is happening in the world because we assume that we are free of bias, photos never lie, and reporters have full access to the truth. None of these assumptions bears scrutiny.

> To discern the truth, we must ask, "How did you come to know that?" and "What's your source?"

To discern the truth, we must ask, "How did you come to know that?" and "What's your source?" War reporting rarely includes firsthand observation. War zones are dangerous. Almost no media outlets want to assume the risk of their employees being present as armies clash. Instead, they purchase reports, pictures, and interviews gathered by freelancers, sometimes called stringers, who are willing to take the risk. If Western reporters do go to the war zone, they are escorted by facilitators who work for one of the warring parties.

In Gaza, these stringers and facilitators report to or work closely with Hamas. This practice was exposed when American media outlets purchased pictures from stringers accompanying Hamas terrorists on their raids, which obviously means that the stringers had to know about the attacks in advance. One of the accused stringers, Hassan Eslaiah, was outed because of a selfie he posted on social media being kissed by Yahya Sinwar, the mastermind of Hamas's October 7 attacks.[170] Complicating the situation, the Associated Press has also covered the proliferation of "deep fake" pictures generated by AI for propaganda purposes.[171] The Israeli intelligence company Cyabra analyzed two million social media posts from early in the war and found that more than forty thousand profiles were fake.[172] According to a source I trust but whose information I could not personally verify, the number of bots designed to promote anti-Israel propaganda could be in the millions.

Propagandists and ethical persuaders alike know the value of pictures. But pictures do not, and perhaps cannot, tell the full story. A group called the Committee for Accuracy in Middle East Reporting in America (CAMERA) pointed out that in a *Los Angeles Times* slideshow of seventy-five photographs from Gaza, there are no photos of Hamas fighters.[173] Journalist Uriel Heilman asked *The New York Times* why they aren't showing such pictures alongside those of bombed buildings. *The Times* claimed to not have any such pictures.[174] Because Hamas's oppressor/oppressed narrative is widely accepted, even by many who find Hamas's tactics revolting, not showing pictures of Hamas's crimes leaves people with the impression that Israel is guilty of those crimes.

> Digging deep and asking difficult questions is the only way to move closer to the truth rather than farther away from it.

Occasionally, media outlets relying on compromised sources will have the integrity to mention it in their reports. More often, they don't. As far back as 2009, the Israeli-Arab reporter Khaled Abu Toameh exposed how Hamas controlled what the world sees in the conflicts in which it is involved.[175] In 2014, Scott Johnson of the conservative *Power Line* blog expressed frustration with American media outlets for not revealing that they "cooperate with Hamas not only in suppressing stories that do not serve Hamas's purposes but also by failing to report on the restrictive conditions under which they are working."[176]

I'm not pointing out these compromises to cast doubt on the brutality of war. I'm not implying that any claims of wrongdoing by Israel ought to be dismissed out of hand. Instead, I'm recommending that we dig deep and ask difficult questions, especially when we think we're sure about what we know. This is the only way to fight the information control that leads to behavior, thought, and emotional control. It's the only way to move closer to the truth, rather than farther away from it.

We have the right to think. We have the responsibility to think. We cannot forfeit this right or this responsibility without partitioning off a significant part of what makes us human. How, exactly, should we think—and act—differently when it comes to Israel and the Palestinian conflict? That is what we will examine next.

CHAPTER 12

What Do We Do Now?

The reason Israel is at war is the same as the reason why Palestinians in Gaza are suffering—Hamas. President Biden noted in a briefing that "Hamas does not stand for the Palestinian people's right to dignity and self-determination. Its stated purpose is the annihilation of the State of Israel and the murder of Jewish people."[177] His statement reminds me of a well-known aphorism among those who support Israel: if Hamas laid down its weapons, there would be no more war. If Israel laid down its weapons, there would be no more Israel.

There are several things we need to consider if we are to think and act biblically regarding Israel and Palestine. We need to recognize the theopolitical reality as well as the geopolitical one. We need to pursue just peacemaking. We need to stand against anti-Semitism and inoculate ourselves against bad ideas in general. From a larger perspective, we need to reclaim the art of conversation and learn how to pray for peace.

Recognize the Theopolitical Reality and Pursue Just Peacemaking

Americans tend to view the world through a political lens. We assume that when push comes to shove, a political solution will be found for our ills, even though we do a poor job ourselves of demonstrating this to the world.

Conflicts that have festered for decades don't get resolved in days. There are no shortcuts. Often, entire generations are born and pass away in the process. We "learn to labor and to wait," as Henry Wadsworth Longfellow put it.[178] Laboring and waiting means thinking hard about peace*making*, not merely peace*keeping*. "Just peacemaking" identifies practices that can reduce injustice and future conflict. Some examples include fostering economic development, supporting organizations that promote human rights, training in nonviolence and conflict resolution, and ensuring physical security.

> Conflicts that have festered for decades don't get resolved in days. There are no shortcuts. Often, entire generations are born and pass away in the process.

Americans generally believe that only a two-state solution will achieve this. If Israel will acknowledge Palestine as a separate nation that has a right to exist and Palestine will recognize Israel as a separate nation that has a right to exist, the problem will be solved, right? Unfortunately, it's not that simple. The idea of a two-state solution has little merit in the Palestinian community. Four times, it has been offered; four times, its leaders walked away. At this moment, Israelis are deeply suspicious of "land for peace" deals, given past betrayals, even though they have agreed to a two-state solution as part of previous negotiated agreements. The rise of Hamas seems to make further concessions impossible.

Even as Israel moves closer to achieving its military objective of eliminating Hamas as a military and governing force, Palestinian leaders are still insisting that "there is no solution except by recognizing the State of Palestine with Jerusalem as its capital and ending the occupation of the land," in the words of Nabil Abu Rudeineh, spokesman for Palestinian President Mahmoud Abbas.[179] This is not a two-state solution. It is a one-state solution that can only be realized if the state of Israel is eliminated.

It seems like the current situation is one that must be managed but may never be fully solved. Managing situations doesn't bring the closure we humans desire, but it can prepare the way for flourishing. This is the reality in other places in the world, such as with the ceasefire between North and South Korea and the fragile relationship between the People's Republic of China and the Republic of China (Taiwan). South Korea and Taiwan have been able to flourish, despite existing in a state of uncertainty. At a minimum, managing the theopolitical reality and pursuing just peacemaking would involve the following:

> It seems like the current situation is one that must be managed but may never be fully solved. Managing situations doesn't bring closure, but it can prepare the way for flourishing.

1. **Open channels of communication.** With the help of trusted third parties, Jewish and Muslim leaders from around the world need to strengthen their dialogue. Itamar Ben David, the intelligence officer I mentioned earlier, says, "The goal is for the children of Abraham, Isaac, and Ishmael to speak to each other." This is complicated but not impossible. In 2020, the United Arab Emirates (UAE), Bahrain, Sudan, and Morocco signed the Abraham Accords peace agreements with Israel. This significant breakthrough resulted in economic cooperation and strategies for confronting the mutual threat they each face with Iran. Other Arab nations are considering normalizing their relations with Israel as well. Palestinian leadership considers this to be a betrayal. But as the opportunities grow, they will be pressured to either join in the conversation or lose what little practical support they have remaining.

2. **Begin developing an agreement that increases security for both Israel and for the Palestinians, including recognition of Israel's legitimacy.** As Jewish author Yossi Klein Halevi admits, "Your side denies my people's legitimacy, my right to self-determination,

and my side prevents your people from achieving national sovereignty."[180] The cycle of denial must be broken.

3. **Exclude Hamas from any negotiated solution and isolate it as a governing or military force.** Based on what we've talked about so far, peace seems impossible while Hamas remains in the equation.

4. **Identify and cultivate Palestinian leaders who are willing to work with Israel.** The leader of the Palestinians in the West Bank, Mahmoud Abbas, is eighty-eight years old as of this writing. He apparently believes he will live into his hundreds and resists turning power over to the next generation. Corruption is widespread in the Palestinian territories. Abbas's unwillingness to pursue a just peace in good faith immensely complicates the Israel/Palestine situation. With the help of Arab nations with which Israel is now developing relations, perhaps there is a path by which new leaders can be identified who will work for a peaceful solution.

5. **Rebuild Gaza through international investment, both governmental and business.** As Hamas is neutralized, negotiators could use international incentives to encourage Palestinian leaders to step back from the brink. This probably will require a new Palestinian leader who has the courage to sign a peace agreement with Israel. The West will need to curb its infatuation with anti-Israel BDS (boycott, divest, and sanction), which only hurts Palestinian attempts to develop economically. As journalist Carrie Sheffield puts it, "The BDS movement inflames rather than enlightens global dialogue around the peace process."[181] Rebuilding Gaza will be the work of decades. For it to occur, someone will need to oversee the process to ensure accountability and prevent development resources from being diverted to the building of terror tunnels or the enrichment of corrupt leaders, as has been the case with Hamas in the past.

6. **End the Palestinian campaign of incitement, which is perpetrated by Palestinian leaders in general but specifically through Hamas.** As we saw earlier, there has been a decades-long campaign by Hamas, carried out through the education system and propaganda, to indoctrinate people against the state of Israel,

in general, and Jews, in particular. As it currently stands, so many people have become radicalized that it is very difficult for Palestinian leaders to back down on their violent demands.

7. **Improve relations between Israeli Jews and Israeli Arabs.** Of Israel's nine million citizens, two million are Arabs. In some cases, according to one long-time observer our group spoke to, Israel doesn't invest in social services and community development among Israeli Arabs as it does among Israeli Jews. Much progress has been made, but continuing this progress will be critical for maintaining the internal integrity of Israel.

The Palestinians are in a tough spot. Their various tribes are at war with one another. Until a leader emerges who can credibly heal the divisions among Palestinians themselves and formally agree that Israel has a right to exist, any peace process will be fraught with difficulty. Any negotiated solution is going to have to make Israel feel that its people are safe and that it will be able to maintain its sovereignty as a Jewish state. It will also need to address Palestinian concerns about security and economic development. The international community will have to come together in a way that it hasn't since the end of the Second World War.

> Any negotiated solution is going to have to secure Israel's safety and sovereignty and also address Palestinian concerns about security and economic development.

All this seems impossible. And yet seemingly impossible things have been accomplished in the past. In 1979, following four armed conflicts between Egypt and Israel, the two nations came together to sign the Camp David Accords. At the time, Gaza and the West Bank were the primary sticking points, just as they are today. But agreement became possible through frameworks of economic security, military security, opening of trade routes, and economic aid from the US to both nations as certain benchmarks were met.

Israel and Egypt broke through their stalemate by realizing that the enemies surrounding them were a greater threat than the enmity they had toward one another. The peace between Israel and Egypt has held for forty-four years. No one at the time thought that could happen. Nothing about it was easy. It still isn't easy. The Egyptian leader Anwar Sadat was assassinated because of his involvement in the process. As we've seen, though, the alternative to a just peace is a shameful one.

Fight Anti-Semitism

Earlier, I compared bad ideas to viruses.[182] They hijack healthy growth mechanisms to quickly multiply and cause massive destruction. Viruses can't really be killed because they are not, strictly speaking, alive. When it comes to viruses in the physical world, scientists don't try to kill them but instead strengthen the immune system in a way that curbs their spread. The international immune system needs strengthening to combat anti-Semitism. The Soviet dissident and Israeli politician Natan Sharansky offers a 3D test for anti-Semitism: *demonization* of Israel, *double standards* applied to Israel but not to other democratic states, and *delegitimization* of Israel.[183]

Opposing Israeli policies and politicians or opposing some of Israel's actions is not anti-Semitism. Denying Israel's right to exist as a Jewish state or mistreating Jews because they are Jewish is. The Israeli Arab journalist I've quoted throughout this book, Khaled Abu Toameh, explained it to me this way: "Being pro-Israel doesn't mean supporting everything Israel does but supporting their right to exist. Being pro-Palestinian doesn't mean you must be anti-Israel."[184] Unfortunately, for reasons that go far back in history, many of the people commenting on the Israel/Hamas war or the plight of Palestinians cannot—or will not—recognize this straightforward distinction.

> Opposing Israeli policies and politicians or opposing some of Israel's actions is not anti-Semitism. Denying Israel's right to exist as a Jewish state or mistreating Jews because they are Jewish is.

Some of the reasons anti-Semitism persists go back into ancient history. A conversation with Rabbi Doron Perez in Jerusalem helped me see this in a new light. Rabbi Perez is executive chairman of the Mizrachi World Movement, a movement of religious Zionists whose goal is to strengthen the relationship between Judaism and the state of Israel. His two sons have both been involved in the Israel/Hamas war. One was shot and wounded, the other killed and his body taken to Gaza.

In his book *The Jewish State: From Opposition to Opportunity*, Rabbi

Perez explains how three kinds of anti-Semitism arose in biblical times:

- **The Moabites** tried to destroy Israel through spiritual contamination, by seducing Israelites sexually and religiously.

- **The Edomites'** anti-Semitism was primarily one of physical destruction. This group attempted to annihilate Israel militarily.

- **The Philistines'** approach was to deny the Jewish people the ability to govern themselves and have a presence in the land.[185]

All three of these anti-Semitisms are with us today; but the third one—denying the Jewish people the ability to govern themselves and have a presence in the land—is the most "respectable" anti-Semitism among the nations of the world.

Christians in history are partly to blame for anti-Semitism. In the Middle Ages, it was Christians, not Muslims, who were the primary persecutors of Jews. Today, Christians have largely corrected for this egregious error. Protestants—especially evangelicals—hold a positive view of Jews and see them as spiritual brothers and sisters, if not co-heirs of God's promise. Among Catholics, the Second Vatican Council in 1965 repudiated the Catholic church's past treatment of Jews and called for positive dialogue.

The anti-Semitism we see today, though, seems to be an invention of the Enlightenment. It is spread largely through anti-Judeo-Christian education, through anti-Israel policies in the United Nations, and through ignorance or false teachings about the Nazi Holocaust in which six million Jews were intentionally killed because they were Jews. It seems strange to say this, but it is a very serious point: much of today's anti-Semitism is spread through two books that remain best-sellers to this day. *Blood Libel* is a false story of ritualized murder by Jews that is approvingly studied by terrorists and their apologists all over the world. *Protocols of the Elders of Zion*, which purports to be a transcript of a meeting of Jewish leaders and has been proven to be fraudulent, is still widely published, especially in Muslim countries. It has even been turned into multi-part television programs in Egypt and Syria. Hamas leaders referenced it in their first charter in support of their anti-Semitic aims.

Prior to the Second World War, anti-semitic attitudes were common in Europe and in the United States. Some of the earliest polls conducted by the Gallup organization dealt with the subject. According to Gallup, when confronted with Nazi treatment of Jews, most Americans found it deplorable. Yet eight in ten still opposed giving Jews sanctuary in America, and more than half believed that the persecution of Jews was at least partly their own fault.

The American attitude toward Jews in the twentieth century led to formal and informal policies that choked off most Jewish immigration and left Jews vulnerable to the Nazi agenda. Who knows how many people died because of America's short-sightedness, which resided at the highest levels of society and was perpetuated by public figures such as Henry Ford, Joseph Kennedy (father of John F. Kennedy), and Charles Lindbergh? Meanwhile, as latent anti-Semitism kept America sidelined in putting pressure on the Nazis, Adolf Hitler was busy indoctrinating German young people en masse. Though he had failed to win majority support among the populace, Hitler's youth program, which grew from fifty thousand members to two million members in just its first year, gave him the edge. Two million young people constituted only a fraction of the German population. But history shows that it doesn't take a majority to destroy a nation. It requires only the activation of an outraged minority and the acquiescence of the rest.

> History shows that it doesn't take a majority to destroy a nation. It requires only the activation of an outraged minority and the acquiescence of the rest.

According to Rabbi Perez, the evolution of anti-Semitism in history depended largely on who held power in different periods of time. In the Middle Ages, persecution of Jews was largely at the hands of Christians. In the twentieth century, it was a form of scientific anti-Semitism based in social Darwinism that positioned Jews as inferior. Today, the highest source of moral authority is human rights. Among the nations of the world, Rabbi Perez says, the language of human rights is increasingly being used to marginalize Jews and erode support for Israel's right to self-determination.[186] If this is true, it is a terrible irony of history.

Inoculate against Bad Ideas

A friend of mine told me that when he was planning a trip to Israel, his son, who had been raised in church and attended Christian schools through college, reacted negatively: "Why are you supporting genocide?"

That reaction, and the way it was phrased, strikes me as the result of a mind virus. Just as viruses trick the body because they're coated with proteins—something the body finds beneficial—bad ideas make themselves believable by coating lies in bits of truth. Bad ideas masquerade as something harmless, or even righteous. Otherwise, they wouldn't spread. You probably wouldn't be tricked by an idea that explicitly promotes fear, disappointment, despair, or defeat.

For two decades, we've assumed that widespread access to information through the internet would squelch the ability of cult-like groups to control thoughts and behavior. It hasn't worked out that way. Weirdly, the rise of social media seems to have created a new kind of mind control, a cult of the self. Social media algorithms are set up to serve customers more of what they are already looking for. We may sense that we are being objective, but social media serves to deeply entrench our confirmation bias based on the conviction that we are at the center of reality. We tell ourselves that *we* know what is really going on and people who disagree are hapless dopes.

There may be a fix for mind viruses. The research of William McGuire, a psychology professor in the 1950s, showed how bad ideas might be resisted. He suggested the following four steps:

- Articulate the truth,
- Reveal the lies that stand against the truth,
- Show how to respond to the lies, and
- Help people develop strong thinking skills.

In other words, you inoculate people to bad ideas in the same way that you inoculate the body against viruses.[187] To test his theory, McGuire prepared arguments in favor of widely rejected claims, such as "brushing your teeth is bad for you." He organized participants into groups that each had varying levels of preparation, from none at all to a mix of exposure, counterargument, and preparation to refute claims that would be made.[188]

As you might expect, better-prepared participants were less likely to be caught off guard. But one surprising finding emerged: just reinforcing what people already knew seemed to make them *more* susceptible to bad ideas. Apparently, when people encountered bad ideas they hadn't heard before and to which they were unprepared to respond, they found themselves strangely drawn toward those ideas. Some people became radicalized in this way. Others just became cynical and disbelieving.

> You can't ignore bad ideas and hope no one will believe them. You must be prepared to think and speak the truth with minds ready for action (see 1 Peter 1).

The point is that you can't ignore bad ideas and hope no one will believe them. You must be prepared to think and speak the truth, with minds ready for action (see 1 Peter 1).

Reclaim the Art of Thoughtful Conversation

When deadly viruses attack, doctors focus on combatting infection and infusing patients with massive doses of fluids and electrolytes to keep the body from going into shock.[189] [190] This doesn't stop the virus, but it buys time to help the body fight for itself. If people are mind-controlled by an oppressor/oppressed narrative, they internalize a sense of guilt for what they suspect is their own complicity in the situation. People with internalized guilt may be unable to see *anything* from *anyone* else's point of view. This leads to anger and judgmentalism. As Albert Camus put it, "The more I accuse myself, the more I have a right to judge you."[191]

Surely, there are times when it is appropriate to feel righteous anger and to make prudent judgments. But our attitude and approach must reflect *biblical* truth, not just our own perspectives. In 2 Timothy 2:24-25, the apostle Paul says, "And the Lord's servant must not be quarrelsome but kind to everyone, able to teach, patiently enduring evil, correcting his opponents with gentleness. God may perhaps grant them repentance leading to a knowledge of the truth, and they may come to their senses and escape from the snare of the devil, after being captured by him to do his will."

Steven Hassan, the psychologist who helps free people from cults, puts it this way: "With all the cult members I meet I try to remember that they are *enslaved*."[192] When you meet someone who is enslaved, you don't berate them for having gotten themselves in that situation. You try to help them get free.

Here are some ways to patiently and gently help people come to a knowledge of the truth.

Ask questions. Questions help people see the truth by igniting their thinking skills. Here are some examples:

- "What can I do to better understand you and build my relationship with you?"
- "How can I communicate my questions and concerns without seeming critical?"
- "What do you mean by that?"
- "Would you be willing to tell me what you're thinking?"
- "How did you arrive at that conclusion?"
- "How do you know that's true?"
- "It sounds like we have a major disagreement that may take time to work through. I believe by talking about it, we can come closer to the truth. How do you see it?"
- "Have you considered?"
- "Can you tell me more about that?"
- "May I share something I've learned that has helped me a lot?"

The goal of these questions is *never* to make someone feel stupid or even to get them to "see the light." It is to help them learn to make decisions for themselves, to be free from mind control, and to grow.

Remember, at this stage, the goal is conversation, not conversion. Leave the conversion up to God. Your job is to share the truth in a relationship-building way. Remember the truism revealed by psychologist

> The goal of questions is never to make someone feel stupid or even to get them to "see the light." It is to help them learn to make decisions for themselves, to be free from mind control, and to grow.

Albert Mehrabian: 55 percent of our communication is *visual*, through our posture and facial expressions; 38 percent is *vocal*, through our tone of voice; and only 7 percent is *verbal*, through our words.[193]

Demonstrate caring. No matter what you say, you want the other person to hear this: "I care about you; I care about our country and our world; and I care about doing what makes sense." I'm not trying to be a therapist here; but in conversations with thousands of young adults, I've learned that anger and judgment arise out of paralyzing fear. It's not just in Gen Z. Up to 85 percent of the population lives with a sense of impending doom, a classic indication of clinical anxiety.[194] For 70 percent of Gen Z, the top fear is being alone.[195] It's important to communicate, "I am concerned, and I care."

> Blaming and shaming don't produce solutions. Thinking hard together often does.

Get to personally know those who disagree with you. People want to find agreement with those they like. Persuasion researcher Robert B. Cialdini says that in negotiations and sales situations, people who take time to get to know one another have greater success. Discussing a study of online negotiation, Cialdini says that 30 percent of the time, the negotiation fails to reach a satisfactory agreement. When participants share personal information about their interests and families to create a connection, the failure rate drops to 6 percent.[196] Simply being likeable and expressing interest significantly increased the success of the negotiations.

Acknowledge differences. Wise conflict resolution begins with "We have differences, and that's okay." Once this is established, focus on commonalities. "We also have more in common than we realize. We both care about making life better for those around us." Blaming and shaming don't produce solutions. Thinking hard together often does.

Don't be discouraged by resistance. Many people, especially younger adults, believe that if what they say might offend someone or hurt their feelings, it is wrong.[197] It's a misguided belief that stops short many discussions about truth. Resistance can be healthy. It brings energy that helps overcome apathy. It helps counteract groupthink and encourages creative alternatives. At some point in difficult conversations, I try to say something like, "Thinking this through with you makes both of us stronger."[198]

To conclude this chapter, here is a quick example of how indoctrination can give way in the face of honest questioning. In April 2024, Summit Ministries conducted an in-depth poll with RMG Research. We asked eighteen-to-twenty-four-year-olds if Israel's greater wealth and military power made its military campaign against Hamas unjust. Forty-seven percent said yes, and just 11 percent said, "Not sure." Then we asked, "Hamas leaders have become wealthy by skimming international aid designated for Palestinian citizens. Do such actions on the part of Hamas leaders make their cause unjust?" Fifty-seven percent said yes, and 23 percent said, "Not sure." Just one question that cast factual doubt on Hamas caused respondents to significantly readjust their impressions about who was being unjust, and half of those who had expressed anti-Israel views were cast into indecision.[199]

It takes a lot of wisdom to communicate the truth without coming across as arrogant or uncaring. The more I find myself in conflict situations, the more I pray for wisdom. Increasingly, my prayers are less about "winning" and more about pursuing peace. As we conclude this chapter, I'd like to note a specific scriptural prayer for peace that relates directly to what is happening in the Middle East right now.

Pray for the Peace of Jerusalem

While in Israel, our group met Allyon Schwartz, a think tank leader focusing on leadership training for the rising generations of Israelis and Palestinians. The head of his organization was murdered, along with the man's two sons, on October 7. In tears, Allyon said, "All Israelis feel that they have to bear witness." As I reflected on this, I realized that one thing we can do to benefit both Israelis and Palestinians—and, ultimately, the whole world—is to bear witness to suffering. Psalm 122:6-9 offers a biblical prayer that can be a starting point:

Pray for the peace of Jerusalem!
"May they be secure who love you!
Peace be within your walls
and security within your towers!"
For my brothers and companions' sake
I will say, "Peace be within you!"
For the sake of the house of the LORD our God,
I will seek your good.

Amen.

CHAPTER 13

Lessons in **Resilience** and **Hope**

During my wartime trip to Israel, many in our group found ourselves asking the leaders we met, "Where is the hope?" So many people are dead. Israel's economy is gutted. The infrastructure of Gaza is destroyed. Amid the pain, we were surprised to hear each one of them express a quiet confidence and determination to rebuild.

I've always thought it odd that surrounded by enemies and under constant attack, Israel is one of the happiest nations in the world. In fact, it is fourth on the list. The United States is fifteenth.[200] Israelis feel a sense of mission for maintaining and strengthening their nation. When air raid sirens sound, they take shelter in safe rooms but then emerge and resume living. When I asked about this, many Israelis distinguished between optimism and hope. Optimism is a good feeling about something; hope is a willingness to act. Optimism is a passive virtue; hope

is an active one. The respected rabbi Jonathan Sacks wrote, "To be a Jew is to be an
agent of hope. Every ritual, every command,
every syllable of the Jewish story is a protest
against escapism, resignation, and the blind
acceptance of fate."[201]

"Life is stronger
than death; hope is
greater than despair."
–Rabbi Daron Perez

Rabbi Perez, whose own son was killed in the Israel/Gaza war, said,
"Life is stronger than death; hope is greater than despair."

One example of this hope was the testimony of journalist Amir
Tibon. On October 7, Amir, his wife, and their two small children hud-
dled in the saferoom of their home in the Nahal Oz kibbutz, the very
kibbutz where Roi Rotberg was killed in 1956 and where Moshe Dayan
gave his famous speech. After the attack, the Tibons found thirty bullet holes in their home and damage from the detonation of a grenade.
Despite this, Amir was determined to return and rebuild his home.

In our group meeting with Amir, I asked, "As an American, I have to
say that I don't know many Americans who would return. Why go back?"

Amir and I have divergent worldviews. He is a leftist progressive;
I'm a conservative. He is secular; I am a believer. Yet I was struck by his
answer. He told our group that his family sees returning to Nahal Oz
as a mission. The mission of Israel is to protect the Jewish people of the
world, he said, and the mission of his kibbutz is
to protect the borders and show the terrorists that
they have not won.

Faithful
presence is the
main way that
people of a
Judeo-Christian
faith hold back
evil and bring
flourishing to
the world.

"But you don't bear arms against the enemy.
How do you fight?" I asked.

He replied, "We fight through our presence."

Faithful presence is the main way that people of a Judeo-Christian faith hold back evil and
bring flourishing to the world. No matter where
we come down on the Israel/Palestine issue, we
can cultivate a worldview that affirms and embraces the habit of faithful
presence. Aristotle said that habit is what brings virtue to completion.[202]
We *become* the thoughts we habitually have chiseled into the granite of
daily life practice. Faithful presence means sacrificing today's comfort
for tomorrow's benefit. It takes vision, and our vision is clearer when we
stand on the elevated platform of core biblical truths: we are deeply loved

by God. Hurt will not win. Our lives have meaning. Even though it is hard, we can seek peace and pursue it in the hope that what is right and just and true will win.

We really have no choice. As an American, I live in a huge country and sometimes entertain the illusion that if I run into trouble in my town, I can just move. This isn't an option in Israel. Come to think of it, though, fleeing isn't really an option anywhere. As Rabbi Perez put it in our meeting, "You can't run away because you are always taking yourself with you."

After returning from Israel, my subconscious mind processed through what I had seen: war-torn communities, traumatized survivors and hostage families, and military members trying their best to restore justice. One night, I had a nightmarish dream of a terrorist attack. But there was a twist. In my dream, I was the one shooting. I was the one throwing grenades into a vehicle to burn those inside. I awoke, startled, crying out, "Christ, have mercy!" I realized that short of the work of God in my life, I, too, am capable of great evil. The more convinced I become of my own purity, the less I understand of reality and the more incapable I become of acting with faithful presence in the world.

"This is the way, walk in it," God says (Isaiah 30:21). Zechariah 8:16-17 offers a sound guideline for how: "'These are the things you must do: Speak truth to one another; make true and sound decisions within your city gates. Do not plot evil in your hearts against your neighbor, and do not love perjury, for I hate all this'—this is the Lord's declaration" (CSB).

Personally, in addition to using my time and financial resources to seek the truth and help those in need, I am recommitting myself to the ministry of prayer. Prayer doesn't replace action; it sparks it. As Nehemiah and his followers returned from captivity to rebuild Jerusalem's broken walls, Nehemiah reminded them, "'Remember the Lord, who is great and awesome, and fight for your brothers, your sons, your daughters, your wives, and your homes'" (Nehemiah 4:14).

Prayer is not about making things easier; it is about imploring God to move in the ways He has promised.

Prayer is not about making things easier; it is about imploring God to move in the ways He has promised. Jesus taught His disciples about the power of prayer and said, "'In this world you will have tribulation.

But take heart; I have overcome the world'" (John 16:33).

As I returned home from Israel, I recalled a line from the movie *The Usual Suspects*, in which the antagonist—a vulnerable-looking, physically-disabled man, said, "The greatest trick the devil ever pulled was convincing the world he did not exist."[203] The bad guy got away because he didn't fit the investigator's preconceived notions of what a criminal looks and acts like.

We ignore the spiritual reality of evil at our own peril. Evil is real. Truth has many enemies. We must not pray for ways to escape the evil but ask God for what we need to obtain victory. God wants to give us everything we need to accomplish what He asks of us. We need to see the world from the standpoint of a bigger truth.

This bigger truth, according to Scripture, is God's kingdom. Christians are citizens of the kingdom of God. We are also citizens of the kingdom of this world. We hold government accountable to fulfill its responsibilities to promote justice and punish evil. We must carefully think and pray through the issues surrounding war and peace and, with a grounding in God's revelation, help both the Church and the state fulfill their respective responsibilities.

Rachel Goldberg, whose son Hersh is still being held hostage in Gaza as of this writing, told our group in Israel that she wakes every day and prays, "I give thanks before You, King living and eternal, for You have returned within me my soul with compassion; abundant is Your faithfulness."

I found it difficult, when hearing Rachel's story, to feel compassion for those who hurt her son. Thoughts of vengeance flooded my mind. I suppose this is only natural. It's easy to be resentful, to think only of punishing evil rather than building up what is good. As Goldberg told us, though, "Hate is easy. Love is hard."

Allyon Schwartz, the think tank leader I quoted earlier, told our group, "The jury is completely out about what we have accomplished, want to accomplish, and are going to accomplish." And yet, he said, referencing Winston Churchill after the Dunkirk debacle during the Second World War, "I am confident that this is Israel's darkest day and its finest hour."

The first part of Schwartz's statement is undoubtedly true. We can pray—and work—to make the second part true as well.

Endnotes

[1] Moshe Dayan, "Moshe Dayan's Eulogy for Roi Rutenberg—April 19, 1956," *Jewish Virtual Library*, accessed April 17, 2024 https://www.jewishvirtuallibrary.org/moshe-dayan-s-eulogy-for-roi-rutenberg-april-19-1956.

[2] Reuters, "Israeli forensic teams describe signs of torture, abuse," Reuters, October 15, 2023, https://www.reuters.com/world/middle-east/israeli-forensic-teams-describe-signs-torture-abuse-2023-10-15/.

[3] Brad Lendon, "How does Hamas get its weapons? A mix of improvisation, resourcefulness and a key overseas benefactor," *CNN* online, October 12, 2023, https://www.cnn.com/2023/10/11/middleeast/hamas-weaponry-gaza-israel-palestine-unrest-intl-hnk-ml/index.html.

[4] Captagon is the brand name for fenethylline, a highly addictive amphetamine that strips its users of conscience and keeps them awake, focused, and calm for days, with no need for food. The drug was found on the bodies of slain terrorists on October 7.

[5] Josh Meyer and Kim Hjelmgaard, "Were the Hamas attacks on Israel so brutal because the killers were high on the drug Captagon?" *USA Today* online, November 3, 2023, https://www.usatoday.com/story/news/world/2023/11/02/hamas-captagon-drug-use-idf-claim/71288873007/.

[6] "Israel: Palestinian armed groups must be held accountable for deliberate civilian killings, abductions and indiscriminate attacks," Amnesty International online, October 12, 2023, https://www.amnesty.org/en/latest/news/2023/10/israel-palestinian-armed-groups-must-be-held-accountable-for-deliberate-civilian-killings-abductions-and-indiscriminate-attacks/.

[7] R. J. Rummel demonstrates that more human beings in the twentieth century died at the hands of their Marxist or fascist governments than in all previous centuries combined. See *Death by Government* (New Brunswick: Transaction Publishers, 1994).

[8] IDF soldier in discussion with the author, January 2024. Name withheld for security reasons.

[9] Summit Ministries National Survey, conducted March 20-21, 2024, with RMG Research, Inc. See https://www.summit.org/about/press/poll-college-protests-on-eve-of-passover-gen-z-sides-with-hamas/ for more information.

[10] Mark Penn, Dritan Nesho, and Stephen Ansolabehere, *Harvard/CAPS/Harris Poll* (United States: Harvard/CAPS/Harris, October 19, 2023), https://harvardharrispoll.com/wp-content/uploads/2023/10/HHP_Oct23_KeyResults.pdf.

[11] Mark Penn, Dritan Nesho, and Stephen Ansolabehere, *Harvard/CAPS/Harris Poll* (United State: Harvard/CAPS/Harris, December 13-14, 2023), https://harvardharrispoll.com/wp-content/uploads/2023/12/HHP_Dec23_KeyResults.pdf.

[12] Terry Collins, "White House announces national strategy to combat antisemitism," *USA Today*, May 25, 2023, https://www.usatoday.com/story/news/nation/2023/05/25/white-house-biden-first-ever-antisemitism-strategy/70257423007/.

[13] Deena Yellin, "Tired of hiding: Jews at US colleges face rising antisemitism from left and right," *USA Today*, June 24, 2023, https://www.usatoday.com/story/news/education/2023/06/24/rise-in-antisemitism-hate-crimes-jews-colleges/70346697007/.

[14] Josh Meyer, "Calls for raping and killing Jewish students at Cornell bring police response, condemnation," October 30, 2023, https://www.usatoday.com/story/news/politics/2023/10/30/anti-semitism-threats-police-cornell/71380881007/.

[15] Khaled Abu Toameh (journalist) in discussion with the author, January 2024.

[16] "Dearborn, Michigan Mayor Abdullah Hammoud In A Pro-Palestinian Rally…" Middle East Media Research Institute, February 5, 2024, https://www.memri.org/reports/dearborn-michigan-mayor-abdullah-hammoud-pro-palestinian-rally-city-resistance-biden-must.

[17] "Dearborn…"

[18] Gianluca Pacchiani, "Hamas bigwig rejects 2-state solution, says Oct. 7 'revived dream to free Palestine,'" *Times of Israel*, January 23, 2024, https://www.timesofisrael.com/hamas-bigwig-rejects-2-state-solution-says-oct-7-revived-dream-to-free-palestine/.

[19] Nathan David Cohn, "How much Is Biden's support of Israel hurting him with young voters?" *New York Times*, December 19, 2023, https://www.nytimes.com/2023/12/19/us/politics/biden-israel-gaza-poll.html.

[20] Numbers 6:24-26

[21] Isaiah 53:6

[22] Alexandr Solzhenitsyn, *The Gulag Archipelago 1918-1956: An Experiment in Literary Investigation* (New York: Harper and Row, 1973), 168.

[23] "Islamic Extremism: Common Concern for Muslim and Western Publics," Pew Research Center, July 14, 2005, https://www.pewresearch.org/global/2005/07/14/i-how-muslims-and-westerners-see-each-other/, accessed February 28, 2024.

[24] "UN General Assembly condemns Israel 14 times in 2023, rest of world 7," *UN Watch*, December 20, 2023, https://unwatch.org/un-general-assembly-condemns-israel-14-times-in-2023-rest-of-world-7/.

[25] Luke Tress, "UN condemned Israel more than all other countries combined in 2022—monitor," January 3, 2023, https://www.timesofisrael.com/un-condemned-israel-more-than-all-other-countries-combined-in-2022-monitor/.

[26] Eric Nelson, *The Hebrew Republic: Jewish Sources and the Transformation of European Political Thought* (Cambridge: Harvard University Press, 2011).

[27] Christopher Write, *Old Testament Ethics for the People of God* (Downers Grove: InterVarsity, 2004), 237.

[28] Paul Johnson, *A History of the Jews* (London: Weidenfeld and Nicolson, 1987), 586.

[29] Jonathan Sacks, "The Challenge of Jewish Leadership," The Rabbi Sacks Legacy Trust, accessed March 5, 2024, https://rabbisacks.org/covenant-conversation/shemot/jewish-leadership/.

[30] This statistic is among developed nations in the world based on its productivity, inflation level, stock market performance, and government debt. See Sharon Wrobel, "Israel ranked 4th-best-performing economy among OECD countries in 2022," *The Times of Israel*, December 26, 2022, https://www.timesofisrael.com/israel-ranked-4th-best-performing-economy-among-oecd-countries-in-2022/amp/.

[31] Jonathan Sacks, *Future Tense: Judaism and Israel in the Twenty-First Century* (New York: Schocken Books, 2009), 16.

[32] Eric Patterson (leading expert on Just War Theory) in discussion with the author, February 17, 2024.

[33] Rebecca Sugar, "Hamas's Agricultural Terrorism," *Wall Street Journal* online, February 26, 2024, https://www.wsj.com/articles/hamas-agricultural-terrorism-oct-7-israel-food-supply-trying-to-break-the-community-e4d91a71.

[34] Laura Silver and Moira Fagan, "Most Israelis Express Confidence in Biden, But His Ratings Are Down from Trump's," July 11, 2022, Pew Research Center, https://www.pewresearch.org/global/2022/07/11/american-views-of-israel/.

[35] Jordan Muchnick and Elaine Kamarck, "Commentary: The generation gap in opinions toward Israel," Brookings Institution, https://www.brookings.edu/articles/the-generation-gap-in-opinions-toward-israel/.

[36] "World Watch List 2024," Open*Doors*, accessed March 27, 2024, https://www.opendoors.org/en-US/persecution/countries/.

[37] Irenaeus, *Against Heresies*, quoted in Michael Allen Williams, *Rethinking "Gnosticism": An Argument for Dismantling a Dubious Category* (Princeton: Princeton University Press, 1996), 52, 121.

[38] See also Rodney Stark, *Cities of God: The Real Story of How Christianity Became an Urban Movement and Conquered Rome* (New York: HarperOne, 2007), 146-48.

[39] For a short primer on replacement theology and various forms of supersessionism, see Michael J. Vlach, "Various forms of replacement theology," *The Masters Seminary Journal* 20, no. 1 (Spring 2009): 57-69, https://tms.edu/wp-content/uploads/2021/09/tmsj20d.pdf.

[40] See Os Guinness, *The Magna Carta of Humanity: Sinai's Revolutionary Faith and the Future of Freedom* (Downers Grove: InterVarsity, 2021), 9.

[41] Wilfred M. McClay, *Land of Hope: An Invitation to the Great American Story* (New York: Encounter Books, 2019), 65.

[42] "National Students for Justice in Palestine," Influence Watch, accessed February 28, 2024, https://www.influencewatch.org/non-profit/national-students-for-justice-in-palestine/.

[43] Shibley Telhami, "As Israel increasingly relies on US evangelicals for support, younger ones are walking away: What polls show," The Brookings Institution, May 26, 2021, https://www.brookings.edu/articles/as-israel-increasingly-relies-on-us-evangelicals-for-support-younger-ones-are-walking-away-what-polls-show/.

[44] Blaise Malley, "Forget the shot and chaser, Gen Z got the Iraq War hangover," *Responsible Statecraft*, March 20, 2023, https://responsiblestatecraft.org/2023/03/20/forget-the-shot-and-chaser-gen-z-got-the-iraq-war-hangover/.

[45] Benjamin Weinthal, "Hamas' recent battle cry for violence against US latest in litany of threats," JINSA, December 30, 2023, https://jinsa.org/hamas-battlecry-for-violence-foxnews-dec30/.

[46] C.S. Lewis, The Screwtape Letters (London: Geoffrey Bles, 1942).

[47] Jay Greene, Albert Cheng, and Ian Kingsbury, "Are Educated People More Anti-Semitic?" *Tablet Magazine*, March 29, 2021, https://www.tabletmag.com/sections/news/articles/are-educated-people-more-anti-semitic-jay-greene-albert-cheng-ian-kingsbury.

[48] Mark Roseman, *The Villa, the Lake, the Meeting: Wannsee and the Final Solution* (London: Allen Lane/Penguin, 2002).

[49] David Breese, *Seven Men Who Rule the World from the Grave* (Chicago: Moody, 1990).

[50] Dale Ahlquist, "Lecture 46: The incredulity of Father Brown," The Society of G.K. Chesterton, accessed April 8, 2024, https://www.chesterton.org/lecture-46/.

[51] Marvin Olasky, "What is Biblical objectivity?: An excerpt from *Reforming Journalism*," *World Magazine*, September 28, 2019, https://wng.org/roundups/what-is-biblical-objectivity-1617225573.

[52] Matthew Arnold, "Dover Beach,." Poetry Foundation, 2024, https://www.poetryfoundation.org/poems/43588/dover-beach.

[53] For biblical passages about working and sharing, see Ephesians 4:28, Hebrews 13:16, Isaiah 58:7, 1 Timothy 6:18, 1 Peter 4:9, 2 Corinthians 8:14, and Psalm 112:9. As opposed to these passages, Marxism demands that wealth be redistributed by force and that private property be abolished.

[54] There are many differences between religions such as Buddhism, Hinduism, Taoism, Shinto, and Confucianism (and Western religions such as New Age thought, Wicca, neo-paganism, and Scientology), so grouping them together seems a little unfair. But each view is pantheistic, which comes from two Greek words, *pan*, which means "all," and *theos*, which means "god." All is god. Everything that exists is one thing.

[55] "Median Income by Country 2024," World Population Review, accessed February 28, 2024, https://worldpopulationreview.com/country-rankings/median-income-by-country.

[56] Geert Wilders, *Marked for Death* (Washington, DC: Regnery, 2012), 113.

[57] John L. Esposito and Dalia Mogahed, "What Makes a Muslim Radical?" *Foreign Policy*, November 2006, http://media.gallup.com/WorldPoll/PDF/MWSRRadical022207.pdf.

[58] John L. Esposito and Dalia Mogahed

[59] John L. Esposito and Dalia Mogahed

[60] M. Zuhdi Jasser, *A Battle for the Soul of Islam* (New York: Threshold Editions, 2012).

[61] When I quote from the Qur'an, I primarily use the translation of A. Yusuf Ali. It is an older translation (sounding much like the King James Version of the Bible) but one

that is well-respected and widely known. See Abdullah Yusuf Ali, *The Holy Qur'an: Text, Translation, and Commentary* (Washington, DC: The American International Printing Company, 1946).

[62] The authoritative source on Shari'ah is Ahmad ibn Naqib al-Misri, *Reliance of the Traveller: A Classic Manual of Islamic Sacred Law*, trans. Nuh Ha Mim Keller (Beltsville: Amana Publications, 1994).

[63] For a detailed critique of Shari'ah from a secularist perspective, refer to Andrew G. Bostom, *Sharia Versus Freedom: The Legacy of Islamic Totalitarianism* (Amherst: Prometheus Press, 2012).

[64] There are 164 references to jihad in the Quran. For more information on Shari'a law, refer to Ahmad ibn Naqib al-Misri, 599-605.

[65] Mark Gabriel—who grew up as a devout Muslim in Egypt, earned a doctorate in Islamic studies, and even taught at Al-Azhar University in Cairo, the most prestigious Islamic university in the world—devotes chapter thirteen of his book *Jesus and Muhammad* (Lake Mary: Frontline, 2004) to interpreting and explaining the Qur'anic references to *jihad* and explaining how it is impossible to logically describe it as merely spiritual struggle. See *Jesus and Muhammad* (Lake Mary: Frontline, 2004), 126-127.

[66] A detailed history of Islamic conquest is available in William J. Federer, *What Every American Needs to Know About the Qur'an: A History of Islam and the United States* (St. Louis: Amerisearch, 2011).

[67] Ahmad ibn Naqib al-Misri points out that "it is offensive to conduct a military expedition against hostile non-Muslims without the caliph's permission." But he further notes that if there is no caliph (Muslim head of a country), no permission is required. Muslims may then wage war as they see fit. See Ahmad ibn Naqib al-Misri, 602.

[68] Nabeel Quereshi, M.D., in discussion with the author, May 2013.

[69] "Preamble," *Hamas: General Principles and Policies*, Jewish Virtual Library, 2017, https://www.jewishvirtuallibrary.org/hamas-2017-document-of-general-principles-and-policies.

[70] "Clause 7," Hamas.

[71] "Clause 15," Hamas.

[72] "Clause 20," Hamas.

[73] "Clause 10," Hamas.

[74] "Clause 23," Hamas.

[75] "Clause 25," Hamas.

[76] Hamas Media Office, "Our Narrative...Operation Al-Aqsa Flood," Lebanon News, accessed February 28, 2024, https://www.lbcgroup.tv/uploadImages/ExtImages/Images2/Our%20Narrative-Operation%20Al-Aqsa%20Flood-Web_compressed%20(1).pdf.

[77] Hamas Media Office.

[78] "ARCCI submits first report regarding Hamas October 7 attack to the UN" Ministry of Foreign Affairs, February 21, 2024, https://www.gov.il/en/pages/arcci-submits-first-report-to-un-21-feb-2024.

79 Qanta Ahmed, "I Saw the Children Hamas Beheaded With My Own Eyes. Shame on Queen Rania | Opinion," *Newsweek*, December 26, 2023, https://www.newsweek.com/i-saw-children-hamas-beheaded-my-own-eyes-shame-queen-rania-opinion-1855472.

80 "Palestine: Impunity for Arbitrary Arrests, Torture," Human Rights Watch, June 30, 2022, https://www.hrw.org/news/2022/06/30/palestine-impunity-arbitrary-arrests-torture.

81 Daniel Eisenbud, "Experts: Over 200 US-approved textbooks teach Palestinians to kill Jews," November 8, 2016, https://www.jpost.com/arab-israeli-conflict/palestinian-text-books-in-unwra-schools-reportedly-teach-of-killing-jews-472012.

82 Daniel Eisenbud.

83 Yaakov Ahimeir, "The Palestinian textbook problem," *Israel Hayom,* February 11, 2018, https://www.israelhayom.com/opinions/the-palestinian-textbook-problem/.

84 Dina Rovner and Arik Agassi, *UNRWA Education: Reform or Regression?"* (Geneva: UN Watch, 2023), https://unwatch.org/wp-content/uploads/2023/03/2023-Report-UNRWA.pdf.

85 Joe Truzman, "Islamic Jihad Begins Military Summer Camp for Palestinian Youth," Foundation for Defense of Democracies, June 13, 2023, https://www.fdd.org/analysis/2023/06/13/islamic-jihad-begins-military-summer-camp-for-palestinian-youth/.

86 Hamsa Howidy, "Opinion: Hamas Tortured Me for Dissent. Here's What They Really Think of Palestinians | Opinion," *Newsweek*, January 2, 2024, https://www.newsweek.com/hamas-tortured-me-dissent-heres-what-they-really-think-palestinians-opinion-1857169.

87 Yossi Klein Halevi, *Letters to My Palestinian Neighbor* (New York: Harper Perennial, 2019), 113.

88 "Palestine, State of," Amnesty International, accessed February 28, 2024, https://www.amnesty.org/en/location/middle-east-and-north-africa/palestine-state-of/report-palestine-state-of/.

89 Muyu Xu, "Explainer: Iran's expanding oil trade with top buyer China," Reuters, November 10, 2023, https://www.reuters.com/markets/commodities/irans-expanding-oil-trade-with-top-buyer-china-2023-11-10/.

90 Kali Robinson, "Backgrounder: What is Hamas?" Council on Foreign Relations, October 31, 2023, https://www.cfr.org/backgrounder/what-hamas.

91 Giselle Ruhiyyih Ewing, "Iran praises Hamas as attack reverberates around Middle East," *Foreign Affairs*, October 7, 2023, https://www.politico.com/news/2023/10/07/iran-praises-hamas-attack-israel-middle-east-00120491#:~.

92 Kali Robinson, "Backgrounder.".

93 Brad Lendon, "How does Hamas get its weapons? A mix of improvisation, resourcefulness and a key overseas benefactor," *CNN* online, October 12, 2023, https://www.cnn.com/2023/10/11/middleeast/hamas-weaponry-gaza-israel-palestine-unrest-intl-hnk-ml/index.html.

94 Adnan Abu Amer, "Report outlines how Iran smuggles arms to Hamas," *AL Monitor*, April 9, 2021, https://www.al-monitor.com/originals/2021/04/report-outlines-how-iran-smuggles-arms-hamas#ixzz8QK1M1Jc9.

[95] Hollie McKay, "A Look Inside Hamas's Weapons Arsenal," *The Cipher Brief*, November 30, 2023, https://www.thecipherbrief.com/a-look-inside-hamass-weapons-arsenal.

[96] Hollie McKay.

[97] Hollie McKay.

[98] Hollie McKay.

[99] Shanine Bruder and Caroline Peacock, "HEIR THIS: Who is in the Qatar royal family and what's their net worth?" *The Sun*, February 28, 2024, https://www.thesun.co.uk/news/20481195/qatar-royal-family-net-worth/.

[100] Rob Davies and Joseph Smith, "How Qatar bought up Britain," *The Guardian*, November 5, 2022, https://www.theguardian.com/business/ng-interactive/2022/nov/05/how-qatar-bought-up-britain.

[101] Kali Robinson, "Backgrounder: What Is Hamas?" Council on Foreign Relations, October 31, 2023, https://www.cfr.org/backgrounder/what-hamas, accessed February 28, 2024.

[102] Rob Davies and Joseph Smith.

[103] "10 Things to Know About Hamas and Qatar," Foundation for Defense of Democracies, December 19, 2023, https://www.fdd.org/analysis/2023/12/19/10-things-to-know-about-hamas-and-qatar/.

[104] Isabel Vincent and Benjamin Weinthal, "Hamas leaders worth staggering $11B revel in luxury—while Gaza's people suffer," *New York Post*, November 7, 2023, https://nypost.com/2023/11/07/news/hamas-leaders-worth-11bn-live-luxury-lives-in-qatar/.

[105] Isabel Vincent and Benjamin Weinthal.

[106] Isabel Vincent and Benjamin Weinthal.

[107] "Hamas's Top Leaders Are Worth Billions. Here's How They Continue To Grow Rich," The Mackenzie Institute, November 3, 2023, https://mackenzieinstitute.com/2023/11/hamass-top-leaders-are-worth-billions-heres-how-they-continue-to-grow-rich/.

[108] "Hamas's Top Leaders…"

[109] Adam Kredo, "Hamas Patron Qatar Has Spent $6 Billion Lobbying the U.S. Government and Funding Universities," *Washington Free Beacon*, February 9, 2024, https://freebeacon.com/national-security/hamas-patron-qatar-has-spent-6-billion-lobbying-the-u-s-government-and-funding-universities/.

[110] Sophie Shulman, "Tuition of terror: Qatari money flowed into U.S. universities - and now it's fueling violence," Ctech, October 30, 2023, https://www.calcalistech.com/ctechnews/article/jwhsqhrat.

[111] Adam Kredo.

[112] Amaney A. Jamal and Michael Robbins, "What Palestinians Really Think of Hamas," *Foreign Affairs*, October 25, 2023, https://www.foreignaffairs.com/israel/what-palestinians-really-think-hamas.

[113] "Poll shows Palestinians back Oct. 7 attack on Israel, support for Hamas rises," *Reuters*, December 14, 2023, https://www.reuters.com/world/middle-east/poll-shows-palestinians-back-oct-7-attack-israel-support-hamas-rises-2023-12-14/.

[114] "Frequently asked questions on the rules of war," International Red Cross, March 7, 2022, https://www.icrc.org/en/document/ihl-rules-of-war-faq-geneva-conventions.

[115] Robert G. Clouse (ed.), *War: Four Christian Views* (Downers Grove: InterVarsity Press, 1991), 120-130. Furthermore, the following work is a classic in the field, though less than sanguine about the possibilities of waging a just war: Paul Ramsey, *The Just War: Force and Political Responsibility* (Lanham, MD: Rowman and Littlefield Publishers, 2002). Arthur Holmes offers a brief historical overview in his section on "Just War" in Robert G. Clouse (ed.), *War: Four Christian Views* (Downers Grove, IL: InterVarsity Press, 1991), 122-30. For further discussion on these criteria and how they developed over time in addition to many of the sources already mentioned and cited, I recommend, David D. Corey and J. Daryl Charles, *The Just War Tradition: An Introduction* (Wilmington: ISI Books, 2012).

[116] Eric Patterson (war expert) in discussion with the author, February 17, 2024.

[117] Rachel Goldberg in discussion with the author, January 20, 2024.

[118] Clouse, 123.

[119] "Sanhedrin 37a," Babylonian Talmud, Sefaria.org, accessed March 13, 2024, https://www.sefaria.org/Sanhedrin.37a.1?lang=bi Sanhedrin 37a.

[120] JC Reporter, "Hamas casualty numbers are 'statistically impossible', says data science professor," *The Jewish Chronicle*, March 8, 2024, https://www.thejc.com/news/world/hamas-casualty-numbers-are-statistically-impossible-says-data-science-professor-rc0tzedc.

[121] Palestinian Ministry of Health, "A Detailed Report of the Victims of Israel's War on the Gaza Strip 7-26 October 2023, Institute for Palestine Studies, September 19, 2023, https://www.palestine-studies.org/en/node/1654513.

[122] Jesse O'Neill, "Hamas official vows to repeat Israel attacks 'again and again' until it is destroyed," *New York Post*, November 1, 2023, https://nypost.com/2023/11/01/news/hamas-official-vows-to-repeat-israel-attacks-again-and-again-until-its-destroyed/.

[123] "Urban Warfare," Center for Civilians in Conflict, accessed February 29, 2024, https://civiliansinconflict.org/our-work/conflict-trends/urban-warfare/.

[124] "Israelis avoiding civilian casualties," Israel War Database, see "Date and Stats," accessed February 29, 2024, https://www.warinisrael.org/.

[125] John Spencer, "Opinion: Israel Defense Forces work to protect civilians—not kill them," *New York Post*, April 4, 2024, https://nypost.com/2024/04/04/opinion/israel-defense-forces-work-to-protect-civilians-not-kill-them/.

[126] Brett Samuels, "'Obvious to us' Israel trying to minimize civilian casualties, Kirby says," *The Hill*, October 31, 2023, https://thehill.com/homenews/administration/4285905-obvious-to-us-israel-trying-to-minimize-civilian-casualties-kirby-says/.

[127] C. Todd Lopez, "Defense Department Continues to Stress Law of War With Israel," November 2, 2023, https://www.defense.gov/News/News-Stories/Article/Article/3578196/defense-department-continues-to-stress-law-of-war-with-israel/.

[128] "NGOs Bolster Hamas' Human Shields Strategy and Cynical Manipulation of Humanitarian Evacuation," *NGO Monitor*, October 17, 2023, https://www.ngo-monitor.org/reports/ngos-bolster-hamas-human-shields-strategy-and-cynical-manipulation-of-humanitarian-evacuation/.

[129] Uriel Heilman, "The images missing from the Gaza war," Jewish Telegraphic Agency, July 31, 2014, https://www.jta.org/2014/07/31/culture/the-images-missing-from-the-gaza-war.

[130] "Hamas isn't the first military group to hide behind civilians as a way to wage war," *The Conversation*, November 16, 2023, https://theconversation.com/hamas-isnt-the-first-military-group-to-hide-behind-civilians-as-a-way-to-wage-war-217880.

[131] Mark Dubowitz, "How Palestinian Terrorists Yet Again Killed Palestinians, Lied to the Media," Foundation for the Defense of Democracies Policy Brief, October 18, 2023, https://www.fdd.org/analysis/2023/10/18/how-palestinian-terrorists-yet-again-killed-palestinians-lied-to-the-media/.

[132] Mark Dubowitz.

[133] "Hamas Official Ali Baraka On Hizbullah TV: We Can Repeat October 7 Many Times; the Mujahideen Stormed the Gaza Envelope and Tomorrow They Will Storm the Galilee, Israel From Wherever They Can," Middle East Media Research Institute, February 5, 2024, https://www.memri.org/reports/hamas-official-ali-baraka-hizbullah-tv-we-can-repeat-october-7-many-times-mujahideen-stormed.

[134] Gianluca Pacchiani, "Hamas bigwig rejects 2-state solution, says Oct. 7 'revived dream to free Palestine,'" *The Times of Israel*, January 23, 2024, https://www.timesofisrael.com/hamas-bigwig-rejects-2-state-solution-says-oct-7-revived-dream-to-free-palestine/.

[135] TOI Staff, "Mashaal: Hamas 'well aware of consequences' of attack, liberation demands 'sacrifices,'" *The Times of Israel*, October 20, 2023, https://www.timesofisrael.com/mashaal-hamas-well-aware-of-consequences-of-attack-liberation-demands-sacrifices/.

[136] "Foundation for Middle East Peace," *Influence Watch*, accessed March 5, 2024, https://www.influencewatch.org/non-profit/foundation-for-middle-east-peace/.

[137] James F. Smith, "Harvard's Growth Lab researchers diagnose South Africa's decline and suggest tough choices to move forward," Harvard Kennedy School, November 21, 2023, https://www.hks.harvard.edu/faculty-research/policy-topics/development-economic-growth/report-state-capacity-collapsing-south.

[138] AIJAC Staff, "Factsheet: South Africa, Hamas, and the ICJ 'genocide' case against Israel," The Australia/Israel and Jewish Affairs Council, February 6, 2024, https://aijac.org.au/fact-sheets/factsheet-south-africa-hamas-and-the-icj-genocide-case-against-israel/.

[139] Nelson Mandela, "Address by President Nelson Mandela at International Day of Solidarity with Palestinian People, Pretoria," December 4, 1997, http://www.mandela.gov.za/mandela_speeches/1997/971204_palestinian.htm.

[140] Mary Kluk, "Opinion |: South Africa's Government Is an Unapologetic, Shameless Proxy for Hamas and Iran," *Haaretz*, November 16, 2023, https://www.haaretz.com/opinion/2023-11-16/ty-article-opinion/.premium/south-africas-government-is-an-unapologetic-shameless-proxy-for-hamas-and-iran/0000018b-d7d9-dffa-adef-f7d979970000.

[141] "South Africa's support for the Palestinian cause has deep roots," *The Economist*, January 11, 2024, https://www.economist.com/middle-east-and-africa/2024/01/11/south-africas-support-for-the-palestinian-cause-has-deep-roots.

[142] Andisiwe Makinana, "ANC says deal reached on billboard debt with Ezulweni Investments," *Sunday Times*, December 22, 2023, https://www.timeslive.co.za/politics/2023-12-22-anc-says-deal-reached-on-billboard-debt-with-ezulweni-investments/#google_vignette.

[143] International Court of Justice, "The Republic of South Africa institutes proceedings against the State of Israel and requests the Court to indicate provisional measures," Press Release, December 29, 2023, https://www.icj-cij.org/node/203395.

[144] "Iran supports South Africa's filing of ICJ case against Israel over 'genocidal acts' in Gaza," *Press TV*, January 10, 2024, https://www.presstv.ir/Detail/2024/01/10/717974/Iran-supports-South-Africa%E2%80%99s-filing-ICJ-case-against-Israel-over--genocidal-acts--in-Gaza.

[145] "South African Minister Refuses To call Iran's Regime Authoritarian," *Iran International*, March 21, 2024, https://www.iranintl.com/en/202403201429.

[146] "Convention on the Prevention and Punishment of the Crime of Genocide," opened for signature December 9, 1948, *General Assembly resolution 260A (III)* (1951) https://www.un.org/en/genocideprevention/documents/atrocity-crimes/Doc.1_Convention%20on%20the%20Prevention%20and%20Punishment%20of%20the%20Crime%20of%20Genocide.pdf.

[147] *South Africa v. Israel*, "Application of the Convention on the Prevention and Punishment of the Crime of Genocide in Gaza," International Court of Justice, January 26, 2024, 17, 44. https://icj-cij.org/sites/default/files/case-related/192/192-20240126-ord-01-00-en.pdf.

[148] "Genocide: Background," United Nations Office on Genocide Prevention and the Responsibility to Protect," accessed March 5, 2024, https://www.un.org/en/genocideprevention/genocide.shtml#:~:text=The%20intent%20is%20the%20most,to%20simply%20disperse%20a%20group.

[149] "Application of the Convention on the Prevention and Punishment of the Crime of Genocide in Gaza," *International Court of Justice*, January 26, 2024, 17, 44. https://icj-cij.org/sites/default/files/case-related/192/192-20240126-ord-01-00-en.pdf.

[150] "Rule 129: Displacement," International Humanitarian Law Databases, 22, 64, https://ihl-databases.icrc.org/en/customary-ihl/v1/rule129#:~:text=into%20occupied%20territory.-,Rule%20129.,imperative%20military%20reasons%20so%20demand.

[151] Awi Fedengruen and Ran Kivetz, "The Data Show Israel Is Not Causing a Gazan Famine," *Real Clear Politics,* April 5, 2024, https://www.realclearpolitics.com/articles/2024/04/05/the_data_show_israel_is_not_causing_a_gazan_famine_150751.html.

[152] Alan Baker, "Amnesty International's hypocrisy and double standards," *The Jerusalem Post*, September 1, 2022, https://www.jpost.com/opinion/article-716009.

[153] Michael Harris, *Winning a Debate with an Israel-Hater: How to Effectively Challenge Anti-Israel Extremists in Your Neighborhood* (Selbyville: Shorehouse Books, 2018).

[154] Warren Hoge, "Group Spotlights Jews Who Left Arab Lands," *The New York Times*, November 5, 2007, https://www.nytimes.com/2007/11/05/world/middleeast/05nations.html.

155 Palestinians who are not Israeli citizens still have some citizenship rights through Israel. They can get passports, access courts and the government, and own private property.

156 Ilan Pappe, "An Interview of Ilan Pappe," By Baudouin Loos *Le Soir (Bruxelles)*, November 29, 1999, https://archive.ph/2012.05.30-162942/http:/www.ee.bgu. ac.il/~censor/katz-directory/$99-11-29loos-pappe-interview.htm.

157 Ilan Pappe.

158 Anthony Pratkanis and Elliot Aronson, *Age of Propaganda: The Everyday Use and Abuse of Persuasion*, (New York: W.H. Freeman and Company, 2001), 11.

159 "Day of Resistance Toolkit," accessed March 13, 2024, https://dw-wp-production. imgix.net/2023/10/DAY-OF-RESISTANCE-TOOLKIT.pdf.

160 "Day of Resistance Toolkit."

161 "Day of Resistance Toolkit."

162 Rich Calder and Matthew Sedacca, "Groups behind Israel-bashing protests backing Hamas attacks got $15M-plus from Soros," *New York Post*, October 28, 2023, https://nypost.com/2023/10/28/metro/soros-funneled-15-m-plus-to-groups-rallying-for-hamas/.

163 "NGOs Bolster Hamas' Human Shields Strategy and Cynical Manipulation of Humanitarian Evacuation," *NGO Monitor*, October 17, 2023, https://www.ngo-monitor.org/reports/ngos-bolster-hamas-human-shields-strategy-and-cynical-manipulation-of-humanitarian-evacuation/.

164 Churches for Middle East Peace is listed as a grantee on the website for the Foundation for Middle East Peace. See "Churches for Middle East Peace," Foundation for Middle East Peace, accessed March 5, 2024, https://fmep.org/grant-program/churches-middle-east-peace/.

165 "CMEP Condemns All Acts of Violence, Calls for Prayer, and Implores Global Leaders to Address Core Issues of the War between Hamas and Israel," Global Ministries, October 7, 2023, Washington, D.C. https://www.globalministries.org/cmep-condemns-all-acts-of-violence-calls-for-prayer-and-implores-global-leaders-toaddress-core-issues-of-the-war-between-hamas-and-israel/.

166 Lorenzo Vidino, "The Hamas Networks in America: A Short History," *GW Program on Extremism*, October 2023, https://extremism.gwu.edu/sites/g/files/zaxdzs5746/files/2023-10/hamas-networks-final.pdf.

167 Steven Hassan, *Combating Cult Mind Control: The Guide to Protection, Rescue and Recovery from Destructive Cults* (Newton: Freedom of Mind Press, 2024), 42.

168 Hassan, 82.

169 Valerie Richardson, "Over 70% of Palestinians say Oct. 7 Hamas attack on Israelis was right decision: Poll," *Washington Times*, March 22, 2024, https://www.washingtontimes.com/news/2024/mar/22/over-70-palestinians-say-oct-7-hamas-attack-israel/.

170 Honest Reporting, "In the hours following our expose, new material is still coming to light concerning Gazan freelance journalist Hassan Eslaiah… whom both AP & CNN used on Oct. 7. Here he is pictured with Hamas leader and mastermind of the Oct. 7 massacre, Yahya Sinwar," X Post, November 8, 2023, 5:02 p.m., https://twitter.com/HonestReporting/status/1722374178991444219.

171 David Klepper, "Fake babies, real horror: Deepfakes from the Gaza war increase fears about AI's power to mislead," *Associated Press*, November 28, 2023, https://apnews.com/article/artificial-intelligence-hamas-israel-misinformation-ai-gaza-a1bb303b637ffbbb9cbc3aa1e000db47.

172 Eric Revell, "Pro-Hamas narratives on social media getting pushed by fake accounts firm says," *Fox Business*, October 12, 2023, https://www.foxbusiness.com/technology/pro-hamas-narratives-social-media-pushed-fake-accounts.

173 Uriel Heilman, "The images missing from the Gaza war," Jewish Telegraphic Agency, July 31, 2014, https://www.jta.org/2014/07/31/culture/the-images-missing-from-the-gaza-war.

174 Uriel Heilman.

175 Khaled Abu Toameh, "Turning a Blind Eye to Hamas Atrocities," Gatestone Institute, August 25, 2009, https://www.gatestoneinstitute.org/755/turning-a-blind-eye-to-hamas-atrocities.

176 Scott Johnson, "Reporting Live from Gaza, Suppressed and Deleted," *Powerline*, July 29, 2014, https://www.powerlineblog.com/archives/2014/07/reporting-live-from-gaza-deleted.php.

177 "Biden's speech: Hamas unleashed evil; we'll ensure Israel has what it needs to respond," *The Times of Israel*, October 10, 2023, https://www.timesofisrael.com/bidens-speech-hamas-unleashed-evil-well-ensure-israel-has-what-it-needs-to-respond/.

178 Henry Wadsworth Longfellow, "A Psalm of Life," Poetry Foundation, accessed March 22, 2024 https://www.poetryfoundation.org/poems/44644/a-psalm-of-life.

179 "Presidency holds US administration responsible for Israel's resumption of aggression on Gaza," *Palestinian News and Info Agency*, December 1, 2023, https://english.wafa.ps/Pages/Details/139740.

180 Yossi Klein Halevi, *Letters to My Palestinian Neighbor* (New York: Harper Perennial, 2019), 115.

181 Carrie Sheffield, "Boycott Israel Movement Stunts The Palestinian Economy," *Forbes*, February 22, 2015, https://www.forbes.com/sites/carriesheffield/2015/02/22/boycott-israel-movement-stunts-the-palestinian-economy/?sh=7534cf191648.

182 Interestingly, the atheist author Richard Dawkins has written about what he calls "mind viruses," a metaphor that is closely related to his concept of the meme, a word he coined in his book, *The Selfish Gene* (Oxford: Oxford University Press, 2006).

183 Natan Sharansky, "3D Test of Anti-Semitism: Demonization, Double Standards, Delegitimization," *Jewish Political Studies Review* 16:3-4 (Fall 2004), https://www.jcpa.org/phas/phas-sharansky-f04.htm.

184 Khaled Abu Toameh (journalist) in discussion with the author, DATE.

185 Doron Perez, *The Jewish State: From Opposition to Opportunity* (Jerusalem: Gefen Publishing House Ltd., 2023), 4-8. Rabbi Perez credits the Jewish teacher the Gaon of Vilna for this insight.

186 Doron Perez, 32.

187 William J. McGuire and Demetrios Papageorgis, "Effectiveness of Forewarning in Developing Resistance to Persuasion," *Public Opinion Quarterly* 26, no. 1 (1962): 24-34, https://www.jstor.org/stable/2747076.

188 Em Griffin, *The Mind Changers: The Art of Christian Persuasion* (Wheaton: Tyndale, 1982).

189 Robert A. Fowler, Thomas Fletcher, et al., "Caring for Critically Ill Patients with Ebola Virus Disease: Perspectives from West Africa," *American Journal of Respiratory and Critical Care Medicine Thoracic Society Journals* 190, no. 7 (2014), https://doi.org/10.1164/rccm.201408-1514CP.

190 T. Eoin West and Amelie von Saint André-von Arnim, "Clinical Presentation and Management of Severe Ebola Virus Disease," *Annals of the American Thoracic Society* 11, no. 9 (2014), https://doi.org/10.1513/annalsats.201410-481ps.

191 Albert Camus, *The Fall* (New York: Knopf, 1963), 88.

192 Steven Hassan, *Combating Cult Mind Control: The Guide to Protection, Rescue and Recovery from Destructive Cults* (Newton: Freedom of Mind Press, 2024), 246.

193 Albert Mehrabian, "Communication Without Words," *Psychology Today Magazine* (1968), reprinted in C. David Mortensen, ed., *Communication Theory*, 2nd ed. (New Brunswick: Transaction, 2008), 193.

194 Jim Folk, "Feeling Of Impending Doom," Anxietycentre.com, accessed March 18, 2022, https://www.anxietycentre.com/anxiety-disorders/symptoms/feeling-of-impending-doom/.

195 Maria Vultaggio, "Gen Z Is Lonely," Statistica, February 4, 2020, https://www.statista.com/chart/20713/lonlieness-america/.

196 Kwame Christian, "How To Become More Influential And Persuasive In Your Negotiations," *Forbes*, May 31, 2021, https://www.forbes.com/sites/kwamechristian/2021/05/31/how-to-become-more-influential-and-persuasive-in-your-negotiations/?sh=71352d6a7ce9.

197 According to the poll conducted in 2017, 29 percent of church-going Christians under forty-five strongly agreed with this statement. Just 8 percent of church-going Christians over forty-five agreed. See "Competing Worldviews Influence Today's Christians," Barna Group, May 9, 2017, https://www.barna.com/research/competing-worldviews-influence-todays-christians/.

198 Eric B. Dent and Susan Galloway Goldberg, "Challenging 'Resistance to Change,'" *Journal of Applied Behavioral Science* 35, no. 1 (1999): 25-41. Dianne Waddell and Amrik S. Sohal, "Resistance: A Constructive Tool for Change Management," *Management Decision* 36, no. 8 (1998): 543-48.

199 Summit Ministries National Survey, conducted March 20-21, 2024, with RMG Research, Inc. See https://www.summit.org/about/press/poll-college-protests-on-eve-of-passover-gen-z-sides-with-hamas/ for more information.

200 Lindsey Matthews and Michelle Baran, "These Aare the World's Happiest Countries in 2024," *Afar*, March 20, 2024, https://www.afar.com/magazine/the-worlds-happiest-country-is-all-about-reading-coffee-and-saunas.

201 Jonathan Sacks, *Future Tense: Jews, Judaism, and Israel in the Twenty-first Century* (New York: Random House, 2009), 250.

202 Aristotle, *Nichomachean Ethics Book 2*, trans. C.D.C. Reeve (Indianapolis: Hackett, 2014), 21.

203 *The Usual Suspects*, directed by Bryan Singer (1995; Universal City, CA: Gramercy Pictures).

Jeff Myers, Ph.D. is president of Summit Ministries, which has trained hundreds of thousands of young leaders to embrace God's truth and champion a biblical worldview. He holds a Doctor of Philosophy degree from the University of Denver and is the author of eighteen books, including *Understanding the Times*, *Understanding the Faith*, *Understanding the Culture*, and *Truth Changes Everything*. Visit www.summit.org.

Summit Ministries exists to equip the rising generation to understand and live out their Christian convictions in today's culture. We help young Christians—and those who work with young Christians—engage today's tough issues such as abortion, transgenderism, relativism, competing worldviews, critical theory, justice, and other cultural ideas influencing the next generation.

Did you enjoy this book?

Support Summit's mission by donating or requesting more books to help share truth with the rising generation. Scan the QR code to get started.